LIVING LOUD ON A BUDGET

AUTHENTIC FINANCIAL LIVING

TANJA GITTENS

COPYRIGHT

*This is **not** a financial advice publication; rather, its purpose is to provide educational content intended to introduce the reader to critical financial concepts and considerations, as well as to compel them to think about their financial futures.*

Publisher: Long Bay Press Holdings

Editor: Letitia Washington

Book Cover Design: Kim + Kay Studio

978-976-97158-0-6 - Hardcover

978-976-97158-1-3 - Paperback

978-976-97158-3-7 - Ebook

978-976-97158-2-0 - Paperback (B&W)

DEDICATION

To the random beings I have met on this journey called life, who have,
in some way, enriched my experience.

CONTENTS

PART III

INTRODUCTION

My name is Tanja, and I am a wanderer - specifically, a *solo* wanderer. I am also a chartered accountant, an introvert, a risk taker, and a money hoarder. My journey to becoming all these things began as a child. In fact, the first memories I can recall, which no doubt led me to who and where I am today, are when I was five or six years old; at which time I decided to *walk away*. To be clear, I was not really walking away. What I mean is, I was making my way home after spending time with adults who were supposed to be minding me but were very busy and taking too long. They had left me unoccupied with two other children, and I quickly decided it was not the best use of my time.

So, I left.

It started as a game. It was the mid -'80s in Barbados during summer vacation, and back then, television programming only lasted for a few hours in the morning and signed off by lunchtime. This meant you would need to find something else to occupy your time or the adults would need to find something to occupy you.

On this day, I was tagging along with a senior member of my extended family, who was engaged in agricultural activities. The two other children I was with, both a few years older than me, decided to make up a random game to occupy our time, something which was common for children of that era when there was nothing else to do. We would individually declare that we were walking home and make our way to the bottom of the gate. We did it twice and returned, but the last time, I did not. Instead of coming back, I walked through the gate and kept going.

I have no idea what was going through my mind at the time, but in a spur-of-the-moment decision, I decided to walk the three kilometers to my house alone. I was about halfway there, when I spotted a vehicle, and being able to read at an early age, I recognized that it was a government owned one; and so, I 'bummed' a ride the rest of the way. I remember being exhausted after that journey, and by the time the other family members got home, I was fast asleep. They did not have access to a telephone and the other children had not raised an alarm to indicate that I did not come back. The adults were acres of land away and only realised that I had wandered off when they returned to the house.

That story sums up a portion of who I was and still am today - someone who wanders, someone who does not need company to take on the open road, someone who will do what they say they will do, and someone who is willing to take calculated risks.

My hope is that as you journey through the pages of this book, you will see the ways in which these characteristics translated to my adult life; but more importantly, my hope is that you will be inspired to Live Loud and move towards authentic financial living.

PART I

THE INNER BEING

CHAPTER 1
MY MONEY STORY
THE EARLY YEARS

As the only child in a family with all working adults and being a well-behaved and mostly silent child during my formative years, I often accompanied them to and from their daily activities. This included attending church seven days a week (with all its extra church activities) and annual trade union conferences.

But my favourite excursions occurred on the Saturday mornings when I went to work with my mother at the luxury hotel, or with my grandmother at the to the supermarket chain where she was employed by a family member.

Both were equally rewarding and fun excursions for a child. At the hotel, I was allowed to wander around the property, even though I was meant to be in one location and not move. However, because everyone knew me, it was never a problem. The staff recognised me and gave me treats. They would take me to their sections of the hotel and show me all the fanciness of the place, while introducing me to their various jobs.

I loved the check-in area, which was in an old, exquisite castle with grand, roped-off furniture. The air conditioner was always on full blast. It was there that the managers' weekly cocktail parties were held and that was the *only* time they would make me leave. I also got to partake of fancy hotel food, which was decadent back then. I met people of many races and nationalities from faraway places and occasionally, as I sat alone in the library reading (yes, the hotel had a library - that was another plus for me), the guests would come and tell me about where they were from. These early experiences confirmed that one day, I would travel to those faraway places; and I already knew I liked plush hotels, seafood, and other delicacies - especially moist chocolate cake and live music. What can I say? I was a child with taste.

On Saturday mornings, I went to work with my grandmother and also found myself wandering through the supermarket, from the main store to the delivery porch. Undoubtedly, one of the highlights of these trips would be the chance to use the machines to price vegetables. Have you ever gone into a supermarket and seen beans labelled as beets? Maybe a child is in the back room on the machine.

The later days, when my grandmother managed the wholesale vegetable department for the chain, were my favourite times, as that was when she would let me write bills for some of the commercial customers. I was allowed to use the carbon copy billing machine, and because she was a perfectionist, I had to focus and get it right. It was there that my love for numbers began (and mostly numbers that had commas and a lot of zeros).

So yes, business and numbers have been a part of me from my early days, and having a love for Mathematics, I chose to become a professional accountant at the age of fourteen years old.

I was not born with a silver spoon and there were no breaks nor favours given to me. I am a firm believer that in life we are dealt a hand, and it is up to us to play it to the best of our ability. When we are seated at the card table, we do not concern ourselves too much with the cards the person next to us has, regardless of how terrible a hand *we* are dealt. Rather, we play it to the best of our ability and aim to win.

Being fortunate enough to understand who I was at an early age, allowed me to chart my path, irrespective of the hand I had been dealt. I knew where I was going, and I knew it would be up to *me* to get me there. I never once felt it was anyone's job but my own, to provide the life I desired. There is also a part of me that never wanted another individual to have the power to decide how far I went or what I deserved.

Because of this, consideration of how hard something might be or how much effort it will take to achieve, rarely crosses my mind. My thought processes usually revolve around determining if the goal is something I really desire, whether it is best for me and then how I will achieve it on my own. The joy of achieving something on your own is an everlasting feeling. It also means there are no debts to be repaid, for nothing in life is free or comes without attachments.

There was never a doubt in my mind that I was going to use education to propel myself into the life I wanted. Whilst we have come a long way as a society (from the days of slavery and when women were primarily homemakers, to the present, with female CEOs and technology that is moving faster than humans can evolve), overnight success may be clouding our judgement. In this day and age, there are many ways to earn a living. Access to the World Wide Web means we can interact with others at the press of a button. Many now choose to debate their personal pathway to improving their lives; however, I firmly believe that the way to catapult your life miles from where you started, is by acquiring a solid education. Whether formal, informal, vocational, or academic, you need a solid, well-rounded education to make it in the open world.

Having already chosen my career path, one that I not only loved (I call it my *first* love), but one I was also good at, I knew I was not going to leave my success up to anyone, and I took control of that by paying for my education. From the age of sixteen, I started to contribute to paying for my book fees and school uniforms by using money I had earned from my summer jobs.

My first official summer job started the last week of my secondary school life. I was given the opportunity and figured that since I was going to go to school and do nothing during the last week, why not go to work and get paid? I earned $200 per week at that job back in the mid-'90s, and every week when I got paid, I would go directly to the bank and deposit half of it. From the remaining portion, I would take out funds to get to work the next week, and the rest was play-money. I realize I was fortunate to be able to decide what I wanted to do with my earnings, as many in my position were not given the choice. Their incomes helped pay household expenses and keep food on the table.

At the end of that summer job, the role I had been performing became available, and the older ladies in the office who had nurtured me that summer suggested I apply. I kept telling them "No", but after being asked for what felt like the hundredth time, I told them I was going to 6th Form school because I had no desire to do the same thing twenty years from then. And that is what I did.

The hand I was dealt included a mostly free education provided by the Barbados Government, paid for by the taxpayers, and to be clear, that is not lost on me. Over my years of travel, I have met many people from all corners of the world who were in shock and awe that I have an accounting degree which was paid for by the taxpayers. This is because many of them are thousands of dollars in debt for degrees they have hardly been able to use.

Whilst the education is free, there are still costs associated with obtaining it, which may seem prohibitive depending on your circumstances. These include general fees, books and the cost of supplies, clothing, transportation, and meals. Not wanting to take the risk of falling into that category of people who still could not afford free education, I decided to take on that responsibility myself.

That first summer job led me to another, which I kept for three years. By the end of that time, I worked more than just summers. I also worked during Christmas holidays and on Easter weekends when they requested that I come in. Unsurprisingly, this job was in a hotel's finance department. During Christmas and Easter, I spent my time in the storeroom updating the computerised inventory system for the end of the financial year end. According to my superiors, this task required a young person. On weekends, I managed the storeroom to facilitate annual vacations.

By the end of those three years, I felt the need to move on, and for my summer vacation job, I was positioned at the head office of (what at the time was) the biggest hotel group in Barbados. By the end of that time, my earnings had increased by more than 200% when compared to the amount I had made at my first summer job, but one thing stayed consistent: I saved half my pay. I once overheard a family member saying to someone during a telephone conversation, "Ya' can't rob she girl. She goes straight to the bank when she gets paid. By the time she gets home, she broke!" with cackles.

Somehow, I managed to use my summer earnings to fund my way to a degree, and for me, it was not all about the money. I was occupying my time during the vacation and getting paid to do so, while simultaneously learning a bunch of things and meeting new people.

I am an introvert who likes meeting and speaking with random people. I just do not want them to follow me home.

During that time, the ability to pay my way through school meant the most to me, but in hindsight, the work experience I gained was probably more valuable. I was a university graduate who had held down substantial responsibility as an accounts clerk, instructed to pay millions of dollars per month in invoices, unassisted, and could actually produce financial statements up to the trial balance stage by the time I left university. I already knew how to use accounting software, manage inventory and record monthly and annual stock taking. I was employable.

In those days, securing a summer job was not easy, but it also was not impossible, as there were not many students who wanted those kinds of robust opportunities. Because of this, I had an advantage. People who chose to work then, wanted to do something simpler and less strenuous during their summer holidays.

I distinctly remember some people in my neighbourhood laughing when I told them I caught two buses to go to work and two to return home every day of my summer vacation. That never phased me, as the other option was to stay home, be idle, and do nothing, as opposed to earning money and spending my days with grown-ups, hearing juicy hotel stories. If you are a hotelier, you know there is never a dull moment in that crazy industry.

During those years, I lucked-out with the seniors I had the opportunity to work with, for not one of them ever declined to teach me whatever they could.

I must also add that early in my career, I met and had the opportunity to work with knowledgeable professionals and sharp accountants, something which many juniors may not have the opportunity to do today in this working environment.

But that is a story for another book...

"Education is the most powerful weapon you can use to change the world".
~Nelson Mandela~

Reflecting on the above quote, I consider that "the world" starts with your immediate situation. If education was going to be my weapon, I could not leave the funding up to the whims and fancies of anyone else. That is the conviction I carried, as I financed my accounting designation as well as any and all personal development skills I have since acquired.

Over the years, I have heavily invested in my personal development, both formally and informally, to fill the gaps left open by my initial education. The education system will not cover all the areas which will allow you to be as rounded as you need to be for this world; and depending on the cards you are dealt as it relates to your home environment, you may have to fill those gaps yourself.

Not all my personal development skills are of an academic nature. I am a lifelong learner who enjoys acquiring new skills. So, over the years, I have formally earned certifications in beauty therapy, dressmaking, web designing and other areas that were of interest to me at one point, but areas that, no doubt, have saved me thousands of dollars over time.

I was partially raised by a traveller and was exposed to travel early on. I had my first airplane ride at eight years old—a trip to Disney World. From that point on, I was hooked on airplane rides and the places they could take me. During those years as a student paying my way through school, the portion of my funds which went to play-money, also included airplane tickets. Looking back at it now, I must have had rubber bands on my money to make it stretch and do all the things I wanted it to do. Either that, or things are simply just way too expensive now.

During those years, a family member would invite me to tag along and provide free accommodation, as long as I paid my own airfare. With air travel costing a fraction of what it costs now, surely, I could afford a $199 round-trip to Puerto Rico. I always made certain I had money left at the end of the summer for a plane ticket and spending money to buy all my clothing and supplies for the next year. There were times I skipped school to go on these trips, because there was no way I would let the opportunity of an adventure with free accommodation pass. By that time, I had already mastered the art of staying home from classes and teaching myself, so it did not matter. I often joke that 'I went to school long, just not regular'. I liked learning, but all the human activity, politics and theatrics were a bit too much for me.

Within a few years of leaving university, and already living on my own, I started traveling through the Caribbean - a week in Trinidad every year on my own and other trips with the service organisation I was a member of. Consequently, my love for travel only increased. During those years, I gained the confidence to travel solo and learned how to do so on a budget, by carefully doing the research needed to plan out my itineraries and costing out my trips paid for in advance.

When I decided to embark on the round-the-world trip during my travel sabbatical, I spent hours researching all the destinations and deciding what adventures I wanted to experience. As part of this process, I created a working budget to determine how much funds I would need for the entire trip based on locations and activities. While I was going to pursue the trip as economically as possible, the idea was not to travel as cheaply as possible, but to enjoy the various adventures in the numerous locations, in the event I never travelled that way again.

After the first day out-and-about in South Africa (the first destination of the trip), it became apparent that I would have to create a system to keep myself on budget. I had spent a few days in London preparing after flying out of Barbados and was already unsure about where I was budget-wise. So that night, I sat down, surrounded by travellers from all over the world making merry, and created a master spreadsheet on my laptop, much to my fellow travellers' amusement. My masterpiece spreadsheet reported expenses in local currency and converted back to my base currency. It also monitored against the budget. I now felt like I was *really* ready to get my adventure on and religiously every day or two, I updated my expenses for the duration of the trip.

During my time on the road, I met a melting pot of people from all sorts of countries, with varying levels of travel experience. Many seemed quite surprised that my itinerary included Japan and

Australia, two of the most expensive travel destinations, and my activities included Formula 1 in Singapore and Kruger National Park in South Africa. Additionally, my accommodation selections included luxury hotels, all on the same trip. The Power of Budgeting!

By living by a budget, I can easily see what my expected expenses are against the allocated budget and can make decisions to determine what is more important.

Of course, life happens, and things do not always go as planned—like being told you will have to move a mountain to obtain a visa for New Zealand and having to drop that destination from the itinerary or being left stranded in Australia for an extra week after New Year's Eve celebrations because of *more* visa issues.

The one money lesson I have learnt from traveling is that a few extra dollars will not hurt anybody. It can be the difference between a ruined trip or a bad day on the road which you can sleep off with a strong nightcap or, being able to afford medical attention, being able to get yourself out of a dangerous situation and the comfort that helps you sleep at night during a pandemic.

CHAPTER SUMMARY

1. What did you want to be when you grew up?
2. Are you on that path or did you choose another path?
3. Are you happy on your current path?
4. What measures can you take to get back on track if you are not?
5. Do you have the skills and confidence to get there?

CHAPTER 2
LIVING OUT LOUD

As you might have realised by now, I have always had a desire to live on my own terms, and this has been the case from a young age. As the saying goes, we only get one life, but if we live it well enough, one is all we will need. I am determined to (and have always been) live life loud, regardless of my financial status. I do not believe that some experiences and opportunities are for a selected few, and with the right choices, hard work, and favour, we can experience this life in a way that is fulfilling to us.

Upon hearing the words *"Living Out Loud,"* one might envision mansions, fast cars, parties, and a flashy lifestyle. For me, *Living Out Loud* has a totally different meaning. To live out loud is having the boldness to live life well as your *true* self, doing what makes you the happiest. To be clear, my version of Living Loud will not look like yours and vice versa. What makes one person happy and truly content will not be the same for everyone, and your version of Living Loud will be subjective, based on your life experiences and personal journey.

A house in which an individual has a bedroom to themselves may seem like a mansion if they grew up sharing a one-room abode, when, in fact, the size of that house may be the outside cottage for others. We are not all born with the same resources and where we are initially planted, impacts heavily on our thoughts and ideologies. However, where we *end up* depends on the life we carve out for ourselves.

My idea of Living Loud is being able to live a life where I am the best version of myself - a life that entails work that is meaningful and rewarding, in a healthy environment with time to pursue the areas of interest I am most passionate about, and surrounded by people whose presence adds to my overall happiness and well-being.

That, in and of itself, sounds like a lot of fluffy words, but if you can dissect those words and break them down into actual habits, you may be able to unlock the key to life's happiness and Living Loud. Despite this, there's no doubt those fluffy words are actually harder to achieve. Not only that, most of us will spend a lifetime trying to do so with only a few feeling as if they have. This is not because it is unachievable, but because it takes introspection and a lot of work to get there.

AUTHENTICALLY YOU, GOING AGAINST THE GRAIN

How Does One Live Out Loud?

Living Out Loud requires being honest about who you are, your willingness to grow, creating good habits, and doing what it takes to get to the next level. It also necessitates the ability to stay focused on your personal path and getting back on the horse every time you fall off until you reach your destination.

In other words, you need to mind the business that pays you, spend your money on the things that matter and add value to you, and not worry about what the Jones' are spending their money on. Only then will you see your value multiply; allowing you to carve out the life you desire.

The definition of Living Out Loud tells a story that it should be unique to an individual and the key is being *authentically you.*

It starts by establishing what your version of Living Out Loud looks like and working towards that goal every day. This is the ultimate version of what you can imagine your life to look like and choosing the path that leads to the happiness you deserve.

If you examine how some people spend their money, one of the common trends you will discover is that there are many who spend based on cultural definitions of success and society's expectations. Living pay cheque-to-pay cheque is often the result of having more bills than pay cheque, and in some cases, a lack of financial knowledge. But occasionally, it is a result of lifestyle choices.

Money lifestyle choices are the ones we make with our daily routines that determine who we are, such as the type of car we drive, the house we live in, the clothing we wear, where our children go to school, and the hobbies we indulge in, and anything that involves how we spend our money.

As I examine the expenses of many people I work with, it is obvious that most of the individuals who are deep in debt find themselves in this position because of lifestyle choices. It felt that an increase in income will correct the issue, but an increase in income will *not* correct the habit of overspending or feeling the need to spend money due to societal expectation.

At some point, stress and anxiety start to take over and people become extremely unhappy with their lives because of not allocating their funds into the areas that make them the most content. Rather, they choose to continue keeping up with others' expectations. It becomes very difficult to get up every day and go to a job they do not really love, to earn a salary and pay for things that, at the end of the day, do not bring true joy.

Living an authentic financial life will take boldness. You must be willing to go against the grain and "do you." You must choose to spend your hard-earned money in the way *you* see fit and do what makes *you* happy. If only I could get a dollar every time I hear someone say, "I wish I could go travelling," or "I wish I could take time off from work," or "work part-time," or "retire early," or "change my career…"

"I wish, I wish…"

Why can't you?

Going Against the Grain

I have found myself in situations where I was going against the grain and off the beaten path several times, especially while travelling. During my round-the-world trip, I was on a minibus with about a dozen other travellers. Everyone, except for me, was headed to the Perhentian Islands, off the East Coast of Malaysia. I, on the other hand, was making my way to Lake Kenyir on the same coast. The Perhentian Islands, with their white sandy beaches, are the travel-lust of many travellers. For a born and bred island girl who has lived on six of them, to date - not so attractive.

I was however, determined to see the largest man-made lake in the world, a lake I only learned existed about five days prior to that. Everyone thought I was crazy for the amount of effort it would take to get there. I was asked if I was sure I did not want to change my mind, since I was only a boat ride away from the islands. I stayed true to my own travel experience and carried on to the lake.

Reaching that lake was one of the hardest travel experiences of my life, where I spent an hour on the street, standing with my suitcase, before I could find a taxi willing to take me the distance of the closest town to the lake. When I did find a driver, he stopped at least three times in the first hour to get the assistance of persons whose command of the English language was better than his. He needed to confirm we both agreed on the price.

In my quest to reach the lake, I did not realise I would have arrived in Kuala Terengganu, the closest major city, on Friday, and that the city was closed on Friday and Saturday due to religious observations. Finally reaching the city late the Friday night, it took another two days of organised chaos, which included people hiding behind cars in an attempt to take my photograph, following me in the streets and all sorts of other madness, before I was able to secure a final journey to the lake.

However, the minute I saw it, all was forgotten. It was worth it and being able to experience those few days there, will be one of the highlights of my travel life.

There were other hiccups I encountered upon reaching the lake, since there were no planned trips scheduled to experience it, but because of this hurdle, I found company in the form of about five other travellers. With effort in numbers, we secured a captain and chartered a boat to enjoy the lake.

Another lesson here was, start the journey. The right company will show up at the right moment.

During that round-the-world trip, I met several people and teamed up with others who were fearful of branching out on their own and not having the experience they would have wished for. While their travel mates wanted to spend their nights in these foreign countries drinking for cheap, and their days hungover, they would rather be doing something more meaningful. As for me, I had not taken a year off work and spent all that money to hang out in bars. That was something which could easily be achieved at home. I had gone to see the world in its true form and rawness, and that is what I did.

There is an African proverb which says, "If you want to go fast, you go alone; but if you want to go far, go as a team." I do not believe that. My experience has been the opposite: if you want to go where no one you know has gone before, then you need to go alone. Similarly, if you want to break the cycle of poverty, stop living pay cheque to pay cheque, earn financial independence, or live life on your terms, you must be willing to boldly do what you have not done before and create a financial life that is built on authenticity.

The road will not be easy. There will be detours, failures, and moments where you question your decisions. There will also be self-doubt and even doubt by those around you; but if you stay true to yourself, stay the course and plow on, there will be a moment when you will sit back and be thankful that you never gave up.

TIME AND MONEY

Some of the wisdom that comes with age shows us that life is a balance of time and money. We start out with mostly time and not so much money (well, most of us), and somewhere in the middle, we have limited time and (hopefully) more money. Nearing to the end, if we manage to live a life that takes us close to four scores, we go back to having a lot of time and (hopefully) some money as well.

There is one small problem with that picture. We spend our most youthful years trading our freedom for money, in hopes of making it to the end with some semblance of health to enjoy what is left.

Life can be a bastard, and the story does not always play out the way we hope. We can get to the finish line with our quality of life so poor that we struggle to enjoy what is left. The numerous hurdles we encounter on the course, leave us beaten up and worn out - or worse, we are not afforded the number of years we thought we would be. If only we had foresight into how much time on this earth we would be granted, I am sure we live a life that looked a lot different.

My personal journey has taken me on the road to find the balance between time and money at every stage of my existence. There have been times when seventy-hour work weeks were the norm, yet I never believed it was going to be my life. Rather, it was a season, and all seasons come to an end. Those seasons served a purpose on the overall journey. They allowed me to propel my career and maximise my earning potential to be able to find the elusive life-balance.

I say *elusive life-balance* because when I started writing this book, I was still working on that concept and did not believe I had yet cracked the code. However, the clarity I have since gained is that, for me, I am more desirous of living a life where there is no need to find a daily balance, but a life where each day I get to partake in areas of all facets of my life, and that is the path upon which I have embarked.

I learned about balance in the back storeroom of the supermarket on the commercial scales. To reach balance, you must keep adding weight and adjusting until you get to the point of equilibrium. The result is compromise. When an object is heavy, you must continue to add weight to the other side to find balance. So, when the workload increases and the deadlines are many, to balance, you must add play or downtime. There are only so many hours in a day, so what happens is you end up pushing your body beyond the boundaries.

On the other hand, if the load is too heavy, you might consider reducing it. That reduction can lead to meaningless, unfulfilling jobs and untapped reservoirs of talent. Sure, we can add activities outside of our careers to add significance that aligns with our true selves, but once again, we need to find balance.

In sum, finding balance is a constant rejigging of the current life load, filtered with compromise, and it gets complicated as there are some pieces that cannot be negotiated or rejigged. In the end, the exercise is musical chairs and not really life-balance.

I now want to live a life that does not entail constant rejigging or compromise or seasons, and simply be able to *live*. Material things are great, and they have the ability to produce fleeting feelings, but for me, there is no feeling like being awakened by my body's internal clock and not an alarm clock, with no demands on my time and the ability to structure my day based on my own whims and fancies.

Once I experienced what that life felt like, while independently being able to take care of my financial obligations, what I valued became obvious.

I recall one morning in Bangkok, Thailand. A few other travellers and I were laughing hysterically as one person in the group was enquiring what and where we were going for lunch. This was funny because we had just walked out of a café, having eaten breakfast.

The blissfulness of an open day where the biggest decision you must make is what you are going to eat for your three square meals must be one of life's treasures. The number of times throughout my career where I have sat at my desk with food next to me and struggled to get fifteen minutes of peace just to eat, is not something I want to remember or ever go back to.

CAREER BREAK

The journey to discovering what my desired life structure looked like started with a career break. To date, I have taken two intentional breaks, and at some other points I was underemployed and maximised that time in other areas.

Of the two career breaks, the first was the travel sabbatical and the other I refer to as *stillness*. Both have served me extremely well and have, in no way, lessened my career opportunities. On the contrary, they have added immeasurable value to my quality of life and mental wellbeing.

In 2010, I reached a crossroads in my career. I had hit the professional objectives I had written on my resume ten years earlier when I left university (which was to be the chief financial person in a large organisation), and I started looking around, asking myself: now what?

The thought of sitting in that chair for the next (insert number) years, consuming stress, did not appeal to me. I started a process of inner reflection, which led me to a question: if I died tomorrow, what would be the one thing I would wish I had done or accomplished? The answer was not a corner office with a fancy title or even a piece of real estate in a highly sought after neighbourhood. It was to travel the world. So, that is what I did.

I took a year off from work and I travelled the world—several months on the open road on a solo trip which took me to South Africa, Singapore, Malaysia, Thailand, Hong Kong, Borneo, Japan, Australia, United States and the United and United Kingdom.

In some cultures, a gap-year is considered a passage of rites, usually taken after university before the individual has had a chance to get stuck in the mundane rituals of life. In the neck of the woods where I grew up, a gap-year was unheard of; however, a self-funded gap-year at the age of thirty years old is no less poignant than one taken at eighteen years old. As a matter of fact, I fully endorse a gap-year at a later age, when one has some experience under their belt and is not trying to find themselves. At this stage, you are more likely to have an understanding of who you are as a person and what you want to experience.

My last break from life was in 2019. I had hit a wall and, recognising that I was burnt out after the worst working experience of my life, I decided to step off the hamster wheel. There was no doubt that I was unwilling to continue down the road of overwork and took some time to figure out a new direction, through a process of stillness.

I am a huge fan of *stillness* and since the onset of the pandemic, I have continued to revel in it. Not only that, but I will eagerly bend the ears of anyone who is willing to listen about the benefits of actively pursuing it.

The objective during this period was not only to recover from the work burnout, but to carve out a path for the next journey. I knew I had come to the end of the current stage of my life, and it was time to head in another direction, but I am always keen on making the next phase the best ever. When you have travelled as many roads as I have, it takes careful calculation and strategy to accomplish that.

My favourite part about stillness is the clarity it brings. When you are moving like a hamster on a treadmill, there are many obvious things you miss because your brain is constantly fried.

The ability to take a career break without the concern of financial ruin, is one of the best gifts you can ever give yourself. The opportunity to use that time to pursue one's passion(s), spend quality time with loved ones, and look after your mental health should be afforded to all.

Unfortunately, the dream we were sold did not include breaks from life, which allow us to look after our mental and physical wellbeing. We earn a 'break' from work by *working*, and that also depends on the hand you are dealt, because in some countries and cultures, taking vacation or time off is almost seen as a weakness. In the yesteryear of life that might fly, but in the world we now live in, with its demands, speed and expectations, it is close to impossible to find a real level of balance.

Let me speak a harsh truth: that balance gets more elusive for black women, who society demands work twice as hard to prove they are worthy of the place they have *earned* (I am aware we are not the only group this pertains to, but I am speaking my truth here).

So, for most, they continue to walk that walk for fear of losing their spot in the promotion line; for fear of not being seen as a team player; for fear of being seen as weak and not up to the task. I choose to not live with that fear, for what is meant for me will not pass me by.

Career breaks have allowed me to fully recharge myself. A western vacation does not allow that. By the time you overwork yourself preparing to get out of the office, you spend the first few days or a week trying to recover. The next week you tackle the to-do list you have been compiling and if you are fortunate to have more than two weeks off, only then does the vacation begin. Before you blink, it is over, or you travel overseas for the vacation and come back more exhausted than when you left. Whatever the choices, the time off just is not enough to enjoy life uninterrupted and mentally recharged.

To be well-rounded, an individual must have time to pursue other paths besides that of their chosen profession. These paths add value to your daily life and can lead to hidden talents which can be pursued either as a hobby and/or new career paths. Career breaks allow for time to pursue these paths without feeling the pressure of the daily grind.

SELF-FULFILLMENT THROUGH LIFE EXPERIENCES

'The Nomad', 'Auntie Travelling Matt' and 'Runaway Pancake' are a few of the monikers I have been given over the years as a result of my travel life. Adventure travel has become a major part of my existence. Coupled with ten years as a senior finance hotelier through the Caribbean, I have spent a lot of my life on the road.

Being on the open road in unfamiliar places gives me immense pleasure. Coming face-to-face with views, people and culture seen only on television or in magazines and books, is what it is all about for me.

There is a famous quote that says, "Travel is the only thing you buy that makes you richer." After twenty years of solo travel, which took me to six continents and over forty countries, I can attest to that. The opportunities to see and experience the many diverse cultures and people of the world, from the richest to the poorest, from communist to capitalist and mixed environments, and the various religious backgrounds, have been extremely rewarding.

The people I met during that time, as well as the experiences, have heavily influenced the person I am today. My preferred travel is what is called *slow travel*. That is where enough time is spent in a location to be able to experience the culture, traditions and daily life of the people. I also prefer off-the-beaten-path travel, shying away from popular and touristy locations, for those hidden spots that provide the true cultural feel of the location. My theory is, we are a product of our environment, and if we never leave our shores, we are limiting ourselves to everything else around us. By spending time with people outside our circle, and by experiencing their cultures, I am able to expand my way of thinking and my perception based on first-hand knowledge, not on what is curated through the media and other sources.

Breaking bread with Cubans as a guest in their homes will forever be one of my most memorable travel moments. There was a genuine contentment of the people that I have never experienced anywhere else, and this was apparent from the first encounter.

I travelled through the country for over two weeks without any prior booking and was completely at the mercy of Cuban hospitality. This was at a time when accommodation was stretched beyond capacity. Showing up in a location with accommodation for only one night (or none) is not unusual with slow travel and is always risky.

This Cuban trip was propelled after the US decision to ease restrictions against the jurisdiction in 2015. The desire to see the country in its pure form was not only mine, but also that of thousands of other travellers who descended—without prior accommodation arrangement.

The morning after my arrival in Havana, the senior owner of the place where I had spent the night, enquired about the plans for my stay. I told him I wanted to make my way to the countryside town of Viñales and he queried whether I had accommodation or transport booked, to which I responded no. He suggested I was too little to be on the open road alone. So, he called his friend who owned lodging in Viñales, and arranged for her to take care of me at her establishment. He then proceeded to call another friend who would secure transport to get there. Every step of the way, wherever I was staying, the owners called ahead and made similar arrangements. This included sending someone to the station with placards that had my name boldly written to pick me up in the next town of my choice, until I arrived back at my original location in Havana. There are many warm stories like this from the various countries I have travelled. Undoubtedly, I am probably still only alive because of a random stranger's actions in some remote part of the world.

One that comes to my mind was the time I was on a moped after dark in Kanchanaburi, Thailand. I was wandering without a clue where I was or how to get back to base after being separated from the group I had started out with that day. I choose to use the word 'wander', as my traveller motto is, "I may wander but I am never lost." However, on this occasion, I may have actually been lost.

Sometimes the travel experience hits a bump in the road like in real life, and on that day, I decided I was better on my own, than with the group I had set off with in the morning to go see the famous Erawan Waterfall (my self-belief has no limit at times). Alas, it was dark outside, the gas needle on the moped (which I had learnt to ride the same morning in the backyard of the lady renting them) was on 'E', and I knew I had missed the turnoff to get back to the town I was staying in.

I eventually called at a house to ask for directions and an older lady who spoke no English came out. After struggling to help me, she called her son from the shower. He spoke a few words of English to direct me, and by some miracle, the directions were enough to get me back to my location. Admittedly, I was slightly annoyed with myself.

Upon reaching the rental shop to return the moped, the owner said, "Where are your friends?" To my shock, I was the first to return, only learning after that the group had split up and struggled to find their way back as well.

On another occasion (yet again, the story started with a waterfall - clearly, I need to stop chasing them) I ended up on an unintentional three-hour hike. I went to photograph a waterfall in Cameron Highland in Malaysia, only to be disappointed at its size. I had read that it was a bigger fall and believed I needed to follow the trail to get a better view.

At some point, it became apparent that the fall was not going to meet my expectations, but I decided to continue the trail, as opposed to turning back and going in the direction I came. Well, that decision was daft, as I was not appropriately dressed for a hike and spent those hours skating through an extremely high, unsecured terrain with a steep drop, in flat sneakers, no other hikers in sight, trying to get to the other side.

Finally making it down in one piece, I found myself in a little village where I managed to use my sense of direction to get to the main road. Because this village was between towns, it was difficult to flag down an empty taxi and get back to my accommodation.

Then I saw a bus approaching. As it got closer, my excitement started to wane. It was the same bus I had taken from Kuala Lumpur to Cameron Highland a few days earlier. It had holes in the floor, allowing its passengers to see the little winding roads that make up the route to the Highlands. I saw my life flash before my eyes several times. The experience was so shocking that after we disembarked and waited for transfer to the accommodation, no one spoke. Everyone stood looking off into space.

Whilst waiting, I took a photo of the bus and a lady enquired why. I told her I wanted to have evidence of the vehicle that almost took my life. It was then that everyone laughed and finally confessed how scared they were. Some even said they had started to write their obituaries every time we encountered another vehicle on the bends of those winding roads.

So, you see, I was not at all excited to see that bus and thought, 'I will let it go by and wait.' But guess what - a black traveller in those remote areas could not hide, and the driver recognised me as having been on the bus a few days before. He decided to stop, and I pretended not to realise he had, but he sent a passenger to let me know they were waiting for me. Now, the entire bus was staring out the windows.

I gave in and got on the bus to a smiling driver saying, "I knew it was you."

To avoid the PTSD from *another* journey, I told him I only needed a ride to the next town, which was about fifteen minutes away. Once I arrived, I thanked him, disembarked, and went to visit a tea plantation.

That was enough excitement for one day.

These types of travel experiences are the ones I take through my daily life. They remind me of what is important and let me know that material things are not necessary. These are the kinds of experiences that let me know I do not need as much as a commercial society wants me to believe. They also let me know that the best way to help someone is by asking them what they need and not assuming I already know. Finally, they convince me that in a trashy world like the one we live in, not *everything* is trash.

CHAPTER SUMMARY

1. What is your idea of 'Living Loud'?
2. Do you believe there are financial restrictions which prevent you from 'Living Loud'?
3. If there were no financial restraints, what is the one thing you would like to do?
4. What plan can you put in place to achieve that one thing?

CHAPTER 3
CALL TO ACTION

During my period of stillness in 2019, I took the opportunity to fully observe the environment around me, and it was apparent that what I was seeing was very unfamiliar. I observed a lifestyle where day-to-day living appeared unhealthy, physically, mentally, and especially emotionally. It was a lifestyle where there was not much time given to self-care and the work hours were completely disproportionate. Add to that the frustrating and exhausting elements of commute and toxic work environments and coworkers who appeared to be on the brink of insanity.

In this day and time, fight or flight seems to be the mode of operation and even people who know better, seem unable to implement mental health care into their daily routines. They are busy trying to survive another day on the hamster wheel. The cost of living has skyrocketed everywhere, the salaries are stagnant, and the middle class is putting on a stiff upper lip, trying to convince themselves that all is well. All the while, they are secretly hiding the debt they are drowning in, as well as the fact they are living pay cheque-to-pay cheque; and oh - there are also the many conversations where persons express an interest to leave and head into unknown pastures and shores, for a chance at a fresh start.

We often talk about the daily struggle, but what I observe has gone beyond that and faces of despair are emerging. It only takes speaking to a few people to corroborate this thought and regardless of their professions, it is obvious that the stress levels are too high. With financial burdens mounting, people are physically, mentally, and emotionally exhausted, and fear of the future is creeping in. Even those who appear to be thriving have trepidation about their later years.

My feeling is that we have moved away from the cultural components which were actually working. Those components included the frugal way we lived, saving money, living within our means, growing our own food, spending time outside, and enjoying the simple things that do not cost money. Instead, we have adopted a fast-paced life which has outpaced us, and many are too embarrassed or afraid to seek the help needed or, they simply do not know where to turn.

We pride ourselves on being resilient, so instead of admitting that a particular path is not working for us, choosing better for ourselves and demanding better of those around us, we keep digging deeper and deeper; but at what point will we finally realise there is only so much resilience we can muster before we end up broken in our bodies, minds, or both?

The joy of life is fading. I do not mean that fake joy we see posted on social media. I mean the immense inner joy, the type we see in children who do not pay bills - that happy-as-a lark joy.

When you live on a small island, it is easy to adopt a small-island mentality where you think this is all there is to life. If everything around you looks the same, sooner rather than later, you accept this 'reality' and believe that this is all there is to it. Six islands later, I can only conclude that it is the same script, different cast; but if you have nothing to gauge it against, it is difficult to see past your circumstance.

During these moments of stillness, I resolved that there needed to be a relearning process within our communities, starting with a process of *unlearning* in order to go forward. While I had not quite figured out my role in that process, I knew, based on my own experience, that one way to take control of your life and subsequently live the one you desire, is through your finances.

FINANCIAL KNOWLEDGE

Then 2020 rolled in, and in the blink of an eye, life as we knew it was turned upside down - this time not for some of us, but the entire world. There was the initial scare, and we were all in it together.

But were we?

The struggles of families to put food on the table and pay the bills and the secret levels of debt that were being ignored (or in some cases hidden from other parties), started to show and skeletons began to emerge from their closets.

As companies started to make financial decisions to protect their bottom line and governments started to ask for pay cuts, questions began to arise. What had been obvious for many years was now coming to light. People were up to their eyeballs in debt, many of them living pay cheque-to-pay cheque (regardless of the size of that pay cheque), and most did not live by a budget (I will never not squint at you when you tell me this).

During this time, we realized we needed to get back to basics. We needed to stock our pantries for the apocalypse and were in our kitchens cooking more than we have in years. We were forced to raise our children without outside help and tighten our belts during those unsure times - all while trying to stay safe and wash our hands.

What emerged from under the surface, was the reality that there is a large body of people who do not possess the financial knowledge to navigate adult life. Further to this, it became apparent that many do not know how to properly adult *at all,* and struggle to even prepare a grocery list to cover more than three days at a time.

It is not possible to get back to basics if you do not know basics in the first place. Many of the skills which were once passed from generation to generation (e.g, cooking, cleaning, maintaining a house, a car, a kitchen, garden, and basic home maintenance, such as plumbing and electrical troubleshooting) are now a thing of the past. When the pandemic hit, people were like deer in headlights.

As company restrictions and restructuring started to play out, the stressful situations got even worse. For some, working from home became working all kinds of hours as they feared being 'chopped'. The stress and strain continued to mount as if the pandemic itself was not scary enough.

One of the key components of managing your financial life successfully is planning, and it is clear that we now operate in a world where most simply waffle through the day without any plan or strategy. The pandemic proved this. At the same time, there were individuals who thrived, not because they were fortunate enough to retain their income (yes, that certainly helps), but because, as one person told me, "I was prepared for times like this."

It is easy to get in your feelings about others who are thriving and there may be a sense of resentment for those who are; but this is not the energy you should project if you have found yourself in a vulnerable position during this time. Instead, you should aim to take this as an opportunity to do better for yourself and your loved ones.

The idea that all we needed was for the world to 'open up' and get back to basics is quite simplistic, as the world we operated in before the pandemic was quite broken and, quite frankly, only working for a small portion of the world's population.

At the beginning of the pandemic, I was asked to be a guest on a podcast on financial matters, which I accepted. It became obvious that people were now eager to learn all they could about financial matters and, most importantly, that they had accepted the need to change their relationships with money.

For many, money is something we do not discuss, and anyone seeking to acquire more can be seen as covetous and not living a righteous life. There are all sorts of stories people conjure in their heads, many of which were passed down to them from the generations before; but whether people wanted to claim their perceptions of money and financial success was another matter. The one undeniable truth is that we all need money to live (that is, unless we go back to the good old days of bartering, and even then, you still needed something to barter). Not only do we need money to live, but a little extra put aside for an emergency, a rainy day or a pandemic really makes the difference in your quality of life and your stress levels.

After several conversations, budget sessions and monthly financial podcasts with individuals of varying backgrounds (mostly women, a few men), here are my thoughts:

1. Financial knowledge is lacking. That was never a secret, but the increase in this information, the introduction of financial literacy curricula in schools, and the creation of mass media programs will not fix the problem, unless the emotional aspect associated with money decisions is addressed as well. Generational myths and societal norms need to be unlearned if we are going to move forward. Most importantly, the financial knowledge we gain needs to be for the current state of world affairs and not from a historical or theoretical perspective.

. . .

2. Today's university graduate is no more equipped for the world we live in than back when I graduated twenty-plus years ago. At least in my case I had already been adulting for several years. It is frustrating to see the young'uns (I have a newfound love for that word), blindly out there trying to find their way, yet we claim to have come so far as a society.

3. The lack of communication in our communities has been detrimental—and not just financially. Light-hearted discussions at social gatherings are in abundance, yet the discussions of substance which need to be taking place are not. I know these conversations are difficult, and I have seen, firsthand, persons say they have no desire to discuss their upbringings and other important matters with younger family members; however, without those stories, they are left to fill in the blanks for themselves. It is okay for us to want children to have access to financial knowledge, but we must understand that those conversations start with parents and guardians. It is obvious that today's graduates still leave schools and universities naïve about what a starting salary looks like. When their expectations are not met, they are easily frustrated, which suggests they have no idea what their parents earn, where they started from, or the sacrifices they endured to achieve what they have. We must also take into consideration that these young'uns are from an era of instant gratification. The period where you can apply for 100% mortgages, supply a paystub, and get $25k (and upwards) approved in two days, and unsolicited credit cards in the mail. The struggle for them is even more real.

4. We are heading into a level of financial uncertainty that is uncharted. Currently, people are borrowing from themselves in the future to live today. This takes the form of cashing out a portion of their retirement funds to get by right now. Older parents are supporting adult children and their families in unprecedented numbers. Children are supplementing the older generation whose pensions have been gravely impacted by inflation, and governments have borrowed money in alarming amounts that are actually scary for the generations to come. Nothing could have prepared us for the financial fallout of the pandemic and what, no doubt, is still yet to unfold; but if there is one take-away from all this, it should be that it can no longer be business as usual. Now is the time to take control of your financial life and actively manage it, regardless of what level of financial security you currently have.

5. Many are suffering in silence without alternative avenues. The financial institutions they have borrowed from may be a source of support for them, but when it comes to creating a concise plan of action to get themselves out of debt or chart the way forward towards the next level, they seem to not know where to turn for assistance. In some cases, they are almost reluctant to ask for said assistance, because now their highly guarded secrets will be out in the open. It is almost as if they have resigned themselves to the fact that their current financial standing is where they are meant to be in life. As a person's perception is heavily influenced by their environment, they can hardly imagine a life that looks different, due (in part) to the fact that they have not seen examples of others who have started from small beginnings and worked their way to a life of abundance. This is a consequence of our culture of silence around money matters. Because our economic history has not been properly documented and there is a lack of meaningful research as statistics and writings relating to our stories and achievements have not been captured, it becomes difficult for persons to access the information or even find motivation if they need to transform their lives.

This is not limited to personal financing. It is also applicable to the subject of entrepreneurship. In most countries, there are organisations whose mandate is to equip people with knowledge to allow them to successfully create and manage their own business.

Many fall short, simply because the theory of business and the real-life environment in which they exist, operate on completely different planets. The real day-to-day of creating and managing a small business in the shark-infested environments of small islands, is hidden behind the doors of the secret society, and the stories are only shared among a few.

It only takes a quick Google search to learn about the financial climate and even current statistics on any of the islands, and it is clear the information is lacking in some areas and non-existent in many. This leaves people winging in the dark. I am told it may not be for lack of research but rather, the slow wheel and the politics of the learned, which leads to the dissemination of this information a decade after it was produced. Whatever the reason, the data becomes useless the longer it takes to be circulated.

Many years ago, I worked with a senior finance executive who would ask the accountant every month if they were a historian. His logic was that by the time the financial reports were completed, the information would only be good for historic purposes, as the opportunity to make any meaningful decisions based on it would be missed.

Much of my findings in the last few years have not been new to me, as I have seen them in my capacity as the head of the finance department in a few companies in the different countries where I have worked. About a decade ago, when payday loans were introduced in the Caribbean, what I saw through the payroll was shocking. These companies were labelled as a 'saviour' to people with small incomes, but the level of dependency that was created did nothing for them in the long-term (I will come back to this in a later chapter). Once an individual starts to live pay cheque to pay cheque, it becomes very difficult to get out of that cycle, and with the introduction of easy access to credit, the situation only got worse.

On the other hand, there have been many occasions when I have sat with a senior team on the eve of payday for the general staff (which totalled two hundred and fifty people in some instances), discussing the fact that we were unable to fund the upcoming payroll. Week after week, month after month, the same conversations and somehow, we always managed to make it happen within the time frame without anyone realising. It was exhausting. I always opined that if people knew how close they had come to not receiving that pay cheque, they would really consider their financial choices. This situation is not exclusive to people on fixed or smaller income, but across the board. The concept that an individual with substantial earnings cannot be financially vulnerable, or that it can only relate to persons with a lower educational level, is flawed. There are many other factors which play into why an individual's financial life is hindering their ability to be fruitful, and I will explore some of them.

As much as we speak about what makes up the composition of a financially successful person, we also need to speak about what hinders that success. Many times, we look at what we need to do, without dissecting the things we are currently doing that do not work. Components such as mindset, teachings, and upbringing, factor in our success and also hinder it.

As explored before, financial knowledge is a major component of our success. What contributes to the hindrance of this success is not so much the lack of this knowledge, but *fear* of moving forward because of that lack of knowledge, as well as the feeling of intimidation with regards to gaining that knowledge.

Admitting you do not have the financial know-how to manoeuvre life as an adult is a hard pill to swallow, and seeking that help can be a humbling experience. While many may want to blame that lack of knowledge on the educational system and their parents or guardians, at some point in time, you must take responsibility for your future. That goes for your financial life as well.

Arming yourself with this knowledge is only half the battle because you still need to be able to practically implement it in a way that will benefit your current and future self. For example, many learn about the benefits of having insurance. It is there to take care of life's unfortunate events and insurance agents will make you think you need every type of insurance under the sun at the highest level you can afford. This may not actually be the best option for you at the time, but with the knowledge you have of all the types of insurance coverage, you can determine which would be beneficial to you and your family. Financial knowledge involves:

1. Knowing how to earn.
2. Understanding how to manage those earnings through a process of budgeting.
3. Learning how to save money for your current and future needs.
4. Knowing how to maintain your finances on a day-to-day basis (i.e., pay your bills on time).
5. Understanding how to research and choose methods of payment and debt options and having the ability to choose debt options which are better for you.
6. Learning how to invest your savings to create more earnings for you in the future.

There are many facets to financial knowledge and with a changing world, there is always something new to learn and another level we can unlock, regardless of how much information we already possess. In trying to get a handle on our daily lives, managing the basics first is paramount. Once we can successfully earn a living and have understood the concept of living within our means, then it is easier to move on to other areas.

There is no point in overwhelming yourself by trying to understand the stock market if you are not earning enough money to pay your monthly bills, for you simply will not have any residual income to invest. If someone has managed to convince you that investing and trading your grocery and rent money is the best way forward, despite knowing you have no residual income, then understand that you are gambling, and there are consequences to gambling.

Adulting financially for the first time can be daunting if you did not have the basics before stepping into adulthood and are now learning as you go along. If the examples you saw growing up were not positive, there are many predators lurking and waiting who can take advantage of your lack of knowledge. They will use shiny objects to entice you and promise ways to get rich overnight. If it needs to be said again, let me say it: there is no overnight success. If something looks too good to be true, it probably is, and if anyone had all the keys to riches, they would not be trying to sell you an idea. They would have unlocked the door for themselves and sailed off into the sunset.

I said all that to say, financial knowledge begins with *common sense*. You must earn enough to sustain yourself. You cannot spend more than you earn, and you must save some for a rainy day. It is simple. Build from that basic knowledge and you will be well on your way. Anytime you get lost in the maze of finances, go right back to the basics.

Revenue minus

Expenses

=

Savings

CHAPTER SUMMARY

1. Do you have enough knowledge to manage your financial life?
2. Were you financially prepared for the pandemic?
3. Do you feel anxious about your financial future?
4. Do you know where to seek additional support?

CHAPTER 4
TRADITIONAL BEHAVIOURS

To put that knowledge into practice, people may need to unlearn some of their traditional behaviours. Traditional behaviours are passed down to us from our ancestors and form the way we were raised, and many times, the way we *continue* to live. What we are not always aware of until we are adults, is that these traditions are not always the best ways; rather they are the best ways that worked during the era of our ancestors, based on the limited knowledge and resources they had at the time. Some of these traditions were projected onto our fore-parents by way of the plantocracy era and now should have no bearing on our current lives. Some of them are the result of plain-old fear.

Let us explore examples of what some of these traditional behaviours look like:

HOW WE SPEND MONEY

1. Working and saving all year to spend all your savings during the Christmas season - because if we did not have new

furniture, new curtains, and food for the multitudes for the holidays, the theory is that we were deprived.

2. Having a specific menu every day, regardless of the seasonality of food or what is available locally. Have you ever told the matriarch of a Caribbean family that the price of plantain was not economical at the time and there were other options in season for a better price? That is unacceptable. Many would never even entertain the *thought* of saying such disrespectful things for fear of reprimand. As a frugal practitioner, you will know that shopping by seasonality is a great way to manage your grocery budget.

3. Assigning feelings of importance to purchases or being brand-loyal, simply because using a particular brand or shopping at a particular store equated to class or richness, while completely ignoring the quality and value of the product or the experience.

4. Regarding preventative health care as something for persons of means and only accessing healthcare when there is a major problem.

FAVOURITISM AND COLOURISM

Colourism is the prejudice or discrimination against individuals with a darker skin tone, typically among people of the same ethnic or racial group. This behaviour originated during slavery when lighter-skinned persons were often shown preferential treatment from the slave master because those individuals were the illegitimate offspring of said masters. Many decades later, this prejudice still sits under the surface in many places and has not been adequately addressed, including in family settings.

There are families across the Caribbean where the expectations of some of its members are different from those of people from the same households. These unfair practices involve some family members not having to contribute financially in the same way as others, or the expectation is that they are to be financially supported. If this practice was because they were incapacitated or unable to provide for themselves, that would be acceptable, but the unspoken reasonings behind this behaviour stems from either being the baby of the family, the colour of their complexion or because they are considered special within the family unit.

'Child A' taking off school early to care for the other siblings was (and still may be) prevalent in some households. Generally, it was the older female child, thereby limiting her ability to gain an education that would allow her to financially take care of herself and her future family.

'Child B' was allocated all the family's extra resources, as it was felt that academically, they were considered above the others. In this instance, all the eggs were put in that one basket.

Then we have 'Child C' who, because of their fairer complexion, was considered the Golden Child. As a result, other family members would pave the way for this child, either bringing home the bacon *for* them or by not requiring a financial contribution from them.

The complexities of these issues create unhealthy money habits for all parties. For starters, it creates individuals who are unprepared for life and who expect that the world will, and should, provide for their needs without any involvement from them. Many times, they are unable to create streams of income to provide for themselves and they, in turn, transfer that behaviour to their offspring, and the cycle continues.

The providers also continue to play the role, which was inadvertently thrust upon them, creating bad money habits for themselves as well, by failing to make the best use of their resources, thus limiting the creation of their own wealth.

Not only are there lasting financial repercussions, but mental ones as well. If persons are made to feel less than throughout their childhood, they can potentially carry that inferiority complex with them through life. This behaviour also rears its head in cultures where one sex is seen as superior and more useful to the family than the other.

While on the surface it may appear that these issues are not as prevalent as they were many years ago, that is not the case. The truth is, it is embedded in the fabric of Caribbean society. At a time when we speak of creating generational wealth for black communities, these are the challenging issues which will need to be discussed and dealt with before we can move forward. This type of learnt behaviour will not self-correct and will continue to be a hindrance to economic growth.

RELIGIOUS RHETORIC

Some of the strongest traditional behaviours are centered around religious rhetoric. Throughout the Bible, there are many passages which uphold the expectations of Christians and their relationship with money. While there are some two thousand passages in the Bible speaking on the subject, the ones most easily recalled from generation to generation are those about greed.

> ***1 Timothy 6:10:*** *For the love of money is the root of all evil: which while some coveted after, they have erred from the faith, and pierced themselves through with many sorrows.*

This Bible verse has been used by many generations to justify why money is a curse to one's life and, in many ways, the part that says "For the love" is forgotten. Instead, it is preached that any abundance of wealth is seen as a root of evil.

Here are a few others:

1. **James 5:1:** Come now, you rich, weep and howl for your miseries, which are coming upon you. Your riches have rotted, and your garments have become moth-eaten. Your

gold and your silver have rusted; and their rust will be a witness against you and will consume your flesh like fire.

2. **Luke 12:15:** Watch out! Be on your guard against all kinds of greed; a man's life does not consist in the abundance of his possessions.

3. **1 Corinthians 6:10:** Nor thieves nor the greedy nor drunkards nor slanderers nor swindlers will inherit the kingdom of God.

This rhetoric has been repeated over and over throughout the Caribbean in many religious settings as a justification for a life of bare survival, sufferation, and the rejection of a path which may lead to any abundance and comfort. This thinking is embedded so deeply in some cultures and families that people feel the need to hide their success, whether financial or otherwise, for fear of being seen as living a sinful life.

Many have been brainwashed to believe that living comfortably is greed. Being able to sleep at night, knowing your bills are paid, being able to provide a safe environment for your family, having access and being able to afford healthcare and overall comfort is not greed. It should be a birthright.

This brainwashing even goes further when people believe that one should not benefit from the fruits of their labour or talents. Oftentimes, you see individuals (again, mostly females) offering their services free of charge, in exchange for a pat on the back, all with the belief they will earn their reward in heaven.

***Matthew 6:19:** Do not store up for yourselves treasures on earth, where moths and vermin destroy, and where thieves break in and steal. But store up for yourselves treasures in heaven, where moths and vermin do not destroy, and where thieves do not break in and steal. For where your treasure is, there your heart will be also.*

Meanwhile, on earth, they are tired, and their bodies are broken from the daily toil and struggle. While that is the life they resign themselves to, their labour is not going in vain. The benefits just are not being shared either with them or the communities in which they reside.

Barbados is considered a religious state with 75% of the population identifying as Christian. It appears to me that beliefs and practices there, are more restricted than those of others who identify as Christian outside the Caribbean region. Furthermore, one cannot help but notice that there is a difference in how money is viewed as well.

During my travel and expat life, I attended several Christian churches of varying denominations, from very small community churches in Guernsey, to a mega church in Hong Kong. From my interactions and observations of persons within these congregations (which, in most foreign countries, included breaking bread after service), the first thing I noticed was that their Christian journey did not seem as prohibitive, and their Christian walk was not scored based on their ability to continue to walk the walk while enduring the struggle.

As I dig further into Christianity in Barbados and the Caribbean to get a better understanding of the thought processes related to money, I am left confused.

Christianity was introduced to the region during the days of slavery through the Church of England, and for a long time was rejected by the planters, as it was reported, "Education and religion will make the negroes better men, but they will not make them better slaves." It was felt it would diminish the lucrative trade of the planters if slaves were occupied in religious sermons, as opposed to tending to the fields (*Slavery and Christianity in the British West Indies, Robert Worthington Smith, 1950*).

John Wesley (whose teachings are embedded in the Methodist movement, which at that time was a branch of the Church of England - one of the earliest adoptions of Christianity in the region), spoke on money in his Sermon 50. His theory was, gain all you can, save all you can, and give all you can. It further expounds on not sacrificing health to gain wealth, living a frugal life and not being wasteful, and that one should share excess with the congregation and others to help in the pursuit of their occupation and callings. How that has been translated to a life of struggle and sufferation is untraceable; however, Timothy 6:6 does say that godliness with contentment is great gain. For we brought nothing into the world, and we can take nothing out of it. Perhaps, that translates to "Little with content is great gain." A phrase often repeated whenever there is any discussion on money or wealth.

PLANTOCRACY ERA

It may be the case that the ideologies of life and wealth are not entirely a result of Christian rhetoric, but also the after-effects of the plantocracy era. Phrases such as *"Poor, peaceful, and polite,"* and *"Little with content is great gain,"* can best explain the sense of inferiority that came about because of this time. If we examine the current social status during the slave era, the three different classes which were birthed from that period still exist. Now, however, they are referred to as the upper class, the middle class, and the working class, as opposed to planters, servants, and slaves.

There is no doubt that the plantocracy era left a sea of damage whose effects can still be felt today. Indeed, many historians of our era have written about it. Not only is the emotional damage which transcends generations apparent, but a study into the debt of many now independent Caribbean countries (all former colonies) can be traced back to the decisions of the plantocracy era and the raping of resources from the region.

The inferiority complex mannerisms and the undermining of identity and values of persons of that era, have resulted in intergenerational trauma, which still exists today. The work needed to correct the curse is hard and taxing. It will take a conscious effort to unlearn a lot of practices which are deemed traditions and to break away from a docile, submissive type of behaviour that prohibits an individual from pursuing their life in totality - a life that sees them being able to utilise all their talents and being rewarded in kind.

In the pursuit of financial knowledge, the effects of the colonial era must be considered, if true financial transformation is to take place. Many of the struggles during the financial journey can be linked to emotional and mental thoughts, as opposed to an inability to effectively manage money. From not asking to be remunerated fairly for your services and products and being unable to save a cent, the *real* reasoning behind these is more emotional, than it is from lack of financial knowledge.

FEAR

The remnants of this era have also left debilitating fear, which prohibits a person from stepping out into the unknown, forcing them to display the submissive behaviour of their fore-parents. This has resulted in most people following the path determined by society, regardless of whether that path works for them or not. This fear is projected onto the individual by those close to them, such as family and friends. Moreover, it will be the major factor for why many people choose careers that are considered safe and do not follow their true passions.

I too, have experienced attempts by others to thrust fear upon me at crucial points in my life. I was warned about being "out in the world and going to unfamiliar lands." I chose to be defiant in my behaviour and responded, "I'll take my chances out there in the world." Twenty years later, the unveiling of some revelatory information regarding that individual's earlier life, highlighted that the fear had nothing to do with me. All I could think was, "What if I had bought into that fear?" I can assure you; I would not be here writing this book.

There were a few times over the years in various countries where fellow coworkers expressed that an office job was far from what they had aspired to do on a daily basis. One person even went on to say that the reason they never branched out to follow their passion in creating a business of their own or pivoting to a field of work they enjoyed more, was because their closest family member had told them most businesses fail. Therefore, in an effort not to cause any friction within the relationship, they got up every day and went to a job they did not care for, and they carried on with a profession they did not like but was considered safe.

When people ask me how I can travel the world the way I do without fear, I remind them, we are not born with fear. It is developed based on the environment we are raised in and the company we keep. If you surround yourself with people who are bold in their life decisions, you will start to believe that you can step out in your own boldness.

Let me tell you a story about lack of fear and boldness, with a hint of silliness.

During my time in South Africa, I spent an entire day on a wine tasting tour through Stellenbosch, where I met two American brothers. A few days after the tour, we randomly ran into each other on top of Table Mountain, where they enquired about my journey onward from Cape Town. I told them I was considering traveling the Garden Route, but was unsure how to make it happen. They suggested I hire a car and drive myself, as they were doing the same; and if they could figure it out without having any experience driving on the left side of the road, surely, I could master it.

I do not know if it was the air (or lack thereof) at that height on the mountain, but it sounded reasonable enough to me. So, I returned to my accommodation, sought the owner, and asked about hiring a car. Without any hesitation, he contacted a car rental company. The representative arrived the next morning, took me to their office, and signed me up.

For the next two weeks, I drove myself in a car with manual transmission without a map or navigation system along the Garden Route from Cape Town to Nelspruit, and then onto Kruger National Park for a solo safari. I had only driven a manual car once since the day I earned my driver's license ten years earlier.

At no point during that process did anyone I spoke to demonstrate any level of fear or try to discourage me. I have, however, spoken to several people since, who cannot fathom *how* I did it, and their first reaction was fear. I am not going to pretend there was not a level of risk with the journey, but like everything in life, we need to make decisions which mitigate the risk—like why we buy insurance.

Just like we sometimes fear stepping into the unknown, we can also have a fear of success. It is not that we are incapable of achieving, but the thought of shifting to another level, moving out of our comfortable environment, or the idea of how others will perceive our success keeps us from pursuing our passion.

It is almost as if the fishbowl mentality needs to rear its ugly head once a person starts to elevate themselves. Whether it is idle gossip about how they achieved what they have, the constant need to remind the individual of where they came from, or the feeling that the person is "showing off because they think they are better than everyone else," is enough for persons to *not* want to break the mould or feel the need to hide their success when they do.

All these non-financial factors affect the way we see ourselves, our earning capacity, and the way in which we spend our money. These factors need to be addressed when we decide to embark on a financial journey, for if we do not, the effort to reach financial success will be crushed.

CHAPTER SUMMARY

1. Do you identify with any of the behavioural hindrances?
2. Can you think of any others you have encountered?
3. How did you overcome these hindrances?
4. Which of these hindrances do you think is holding you back?
5. How do you plan to move past them?

CHAPTER 5

THE MINDSET OF A FINANCIALLY SUCCESSFUL PERSON

Once we have examined the factors that hinder financial success, we need to explore the behaviours and qualities which are needed for one to have a flourishing financial life.

Financially competent persons are individuals who accept responsibility for their own lives by making adult decisions about their finances and future wealth. They do not expect their needs to be met by another individual or the state for free. They are aware that money does *not* grow on trees, and that it is not about how much money they make, but how much of it they keep, and most importantly, allocating it to the areas of life that add value and enjoyment to their present and future circumstances, as well as those around them.

In addition to financial knowledge, there are some qualities an individual needs to possess if they are going to be financially responsible. They include *discipline, focus, consistency*, and (most pertinent) *authenticity*. These characteristics can seem like those needed to be successful in any area of life, and in a nutshell they are. If you can develop these traits, you can easily translate them to another sphere.

AUTHENTICITY

Who Are you? I mean really, who ARE YOU?

Authenticity is one of those life lessons that will continue to follow us until we get it right, and throughout this book, I will keep referring to it.

Regardless of whether we are honest with the world, the one person we need to be honest with is *ourselves*. Financial authenticity involves being honest with who we are as people and making decisions which reflect that. This includes spending money on the things that excite us and add value to our life and not just for the sake of image.

But financial authenticity goes further than that. It includes embracing where you are in your financial journey and not pretending nor projecting. We cannot help the village if we ourselves are struggling. I know this may seem to go against the principles of how we were raised. In my experience, the community expects that, regardless of how little you have, it is always best to share.

The concept of putting *your* mask on *first* was never applied. Buying fancy gifts for family and friends while drowning in debt; giving food to the neighbourhood while your own children are hungry; making large charity donations you cannot afford, to give the impression you are more financially stable than you are, demonstrates financial irresponsibility and not living a true and authentic financial life. Because you cannot afford something right now, does not mean you will not be able to at a later point in life. By acknowledging where you are in your journey and making the best decisions, your financial long-term goals can be achieved.

Authenticity also ensures the financial decisions we make are customised and reflect who we are and our lifestyle. In certain cultures, there is a tradition of going to school, getting an education, getting married, buying a house, having some children, saving for retirement, and living happily ever after. That entire trajectory involves making financial decisions at each step of the way, such as the career you choose, the type of house you purchase (and in what neighbourhood), what level of insurance you need to protect your loved ones, and the level of risk you are willing to take on to achieve your retirement goals. That path assumes we are alike, want the same things in life, and are going to the same ultimate place; but that is not the case.

An individual who does not want a family will not have the same insurance needs or housing requirements as someone with a family. Likewise, someone who plans to work until the official retirement age will not make the same financial decisions related to risk as someone who plans to retire early.

Therefore, we must be honest about our personal goals and current circumstances and make decisions that reflect who we are. As we grow in life, our desires change, and we need to give ourselves the financial grace to be able to mature. We would not want to abort the ability to choose to take a new career path in our forties because we are so financially wound up, we cannot make it a reality.

Authenticity is not always easy to achieve, and here's why. When we are born, we do not already know who we are. If I consider the anecdote I shared in the introduction of this book when I *walked away*, I did not realize this behaviour was part of my innate personality. The truth is, we are moulded and influenced by our environments and those around us. Our families, the community, sporting organisations, and working environments, play a role in impacting our physical and emotional development. Unless we intentionally explore outside those pre-determined environments, we have no idea who we truly are. Some people go from one predetermined environment to the next, without any idea of what their own selfish desires are.

Who are you when no-one is watching?

Who are you without the input from your family and friends?

Who are you when you make a purely selfish decision?

The gap-year concept and sabbaticals are built to assist individuals who wish to find themselves, and we often hear of people traveling to faraway places to do so. Are they really trying to find themselves, or simply giving themselves space and permission to be who they genuinely want to be, without the eyes and judgment of the worlds to which they belong?

How can you find your authentic voice?

Here is something to do. In four lines, describe yourself. Include ideas relating to your likes and dislikes, what truly makes you happy, your ultimate life goal, and what you want to be remembered for. For bonus points, do so without mentioning your career or other people.

That may sound like an easy task, but I am certain there will be many who will not be able to complete it. This will be because they have never taken the time to ponder these questions in the past, or they may not have been allowed to make decisions for themselves. Perhaps they may not have sufficient life experience to know what options are available.

If you are truly living an authentic financial life, your effort, time, and monies will be directed towards those areas you have described in those few lines, and upon reflection, if completing that exercise forces you to realize that your financial life *isn't* leading you towards your ultimate goal and what you want to be remembered for, then where *is* it leading you?

PLANNING

"Life doesn't happen by chance. It happens by planning."

I started saying this phrase several years ago, and part of it may have been due to being told by a friend that I was "calculating" because of some of the deliberate steps I have taken in my career. Ironically, I spend my days with calculators, so maybe I have learnt a bit about life from these mathematical instruments; but the fact is, we are the architects of our lives and if we are not planning and creating them, then who is?

Being organised is a superpower. It allows you to maximise your day to get the best out of the twenty-four hours you have been allotted. It allows you to stay focused because you have a map of where you are going. It also allows you to have the time to simply enjoy life and all the trimmings and not have to run around like a headless chicken. As Dale Carnegie said, "An hour of planning saves you ten hours of doing." Time is one of our most valuable currencies, which is why we need to be conscious of how we spend it.

Creating a budget and using that budget to manage your financial daily life (knowing when the bills are due and setting up the process to have them paid on time, preparing a grocery list ahead of time, having an emergency pantry, preparing for the hurricane season ahead of time and not when the hurricane is on the doorstep) are tasks that, when planned effectively, make for a smoother life and better financial management. When you have those basics covered, you are better able to steer your financial life in the right direction and focus on creating long-term plans which include wealth generation for you and your family.

There is a cost attached to not being organised. *Last minute* usually means an increase in costs. Bills not being paid on time result in late fees, penalties, and a hit to your credit rating. Lack of planning also involves a poor use of one's time, as well as time spent standing in a line on the last day a payment or application is due. It is time that could be better spent doing other things without the added stress.

Planning ahead and the best utilisation of one's time, is a muscle that needs to be trained. If you grew up in an environment that had structure (even structure that was extreme), chances are you will carry that into your adult life. Even when you fall or life challenges come your way, you will find your footing again, because the muscle memory is there, similar to muscle memory that is the result of a fitness routine.

However, if you were raised in chaos, you will have to learn how this works and, like every learning experience, it will take time and practice. You must get back on the horse each time you fall off, until it becomes natural to you.

Financial knowledge and the most advanced educational training do not teach you the benefits of being organised or how to structure your day. In any office setting, it is easy to identify the people who are organised in their personal lives, simply from observing how they manage their working day. Over the years, I have shied away from working with executives who are disorganised and unfocused. As a highly organised individual, I find it very frustrating and counterproductive. Because I have challenges with chronic fatigue, it is not simply a mere annoyance, but it can also have a greater effect on my personal life, and my experience is that most of those disorganised people do not have the emotional intelligence to understand what that inconvenience does to others.

Planning and being organised will lead you to a place called "Boundaries". To maximise your time, you need to establish firm ones.

Now, this is where it gets sticky, as some people see your setting of boundaries as a form of disrespect and not about you being unwilling to over-commit or create a calmer life for yourself. Go ahead and set your boundaries, anyway. The world will adapt. If you are adamant that you do not have four hours every week to discuss invaluable, nonsensical matters that do not bring you peace, people will adjust, or they will simply find someone else with whom to be unproductive. Either one works.

I love to-do lists and create them even for days I do not plan on doing much. This is because I want to ensure I have allocated the time to do nothing. These daily and weekly lists are developed from my monthly goal list, which is the byproduct of my yearly goals, which are derived from my ultimate master plan.

Five years ago, I started creating a goal-setting plan for myself at the beginning of the year. It was really in a quest to find that elusive balance, as I wanted to be intentional in not only achieving my long-term goals, but in not doing so at the expense of other areas of my life. I knew it was holding myself accountable but had not given much thought about how bulletproof it was until the pandemic. That was when I realised I had managed to be focused enough to achieve a large portion of my goals, even while the world was melting down. Eager to see if it was due to the goal-setting system, I created a programme and invited a few people to join the pilot stage in 2021. It is an accelerated goal programme which forces people to look at their life in totality. They are required to create objectives for each facet and work towards those objectives by taking their long-term goals and breaking them down into smaller ones, with targets for the month, year, and further into the future. Time management, budgeting, business development, strategic planning, project management and self-improvement skills are developed or enhanced to higher levels, which highlights the areas in which participants need additional assistance. I have coined it "an accelerated programme" because, thus far, it is my theory that those who are motivated are the ones who will benefit most.

As part of this plan and mindful practice, which I have since incorporated into my daily life, every night I do a brief recap of my day, what I achieved, and where I spent my time. Some days it looks like: I cooked three square meals, had a walk outdoors, and listened to music. That is satisfactory to me, as that may have been exactly what was on the list for that day.

Being organised is not about filling each waking moment with tasks and objectives or creating rigidity in our lives to prove we are more productive or efficient than anyone else. It is about utilising those twenty-four hours of the day in a way that allows us to live and enjoy the moments.

DISCIPLINE

I am not talking about a hard slap on a child's arse when they do not listen or do as they are told, but the kind of self-discipline that makes you get up every morning at 5 AM and go to the gym (...well, those people are weirdos, but you get the point I am making). I am referring to the kind of discipline that wills you to repeatedly carry out a task, even if you are not great at it or fully enjoy it, because you know the rewards are beneficial. There is a reason some of the most successful athletes later evolve into successful business people. They have been able to transfer the qualities that made them great on the fields, tracks, and stadiums to the business arena.

A little under ten years ago, I had the opportunity to attend a conference in Las Vegas, where Magic Johnson was one of the featured speakers. He spoke about how he carried the qualities which had made him great on the basketball court to the boardroom and went on to discuss how he had invested in the underserved black communities, at a time when no major franchises were represented there.

Today, there are many athletes who have successfully transferred their winning attitudes to the boardroom and, no doubt, discipline comes into play. If you follow their stories, not all of them started out being financially savvy, either. Many of them speak about how much money they blew in the early part of their careers, but once that lightbulb moment finally happened, they realised they already had it in them to be as disciplined with their money as they had been with their training.

Let us consider how that same level of discipline and determination can be transferred to your daily financial life.

Financial discipline looks like buying the items on your grocery list (and nothing more) and staying within your monthly budget (and not being thriftless). It also means doing what you need to do, to create the earnings you require to achieve your goals.

Financial discipline can be built over time by a series of intentional actions. First, you must identify the areas that need help and create exercises to implement them. For example, if you struggle with impulse buying, ways to overcome that might include waiting a week before making purchases, which might be called a *cooling-off period* (to determine if you still need the item), removing credit cards from online sites, and unsubscribing from email lists to avoid temptation.

Practicing delayed gratification is a fantastic way to create the self-control needed to achieve financial discipline. The objective is to forego instant pleasure to achieve long-term goals. This may look like *not* using credit to go on a holiday, versus taking it one year later and paying for it using money specifically set aside. It might look like not undertaking a 100% mortgage and being house-poor, versus waiting until you have saved for a down payment that allows you to have a monthly fee which falls within your budget allocation.

For delayed gratification to be successful, the long-term objectives must be enough to keep an individual motivated. To arrive at the destination, there should be a series of small rewards, which will allow an individual to not feel as if they are being deprived. This is not always easy to achieve, especially when we are bombarded with images of pretty things all day, through advertisements and social media reels portraying the perfect, materialistic life.

Avoiding excessive imagery is one way to assist with the temptation, but it may not be realistic to exist hiding from it. What is required is the ability to find joy in *not* spending; that is, finding ways to occupy your time and create a feeling of contentment that does not involve money. Seeking these kinds of activities will not only help you avoid spending, but it can also decrease your stress levels and help you gain perspective, especially if you find yourself comparing your life or progress to others.

CONSISTENCY

When you are disciplined enough to do something every day, it is called consistency, and that is when you will see results. To be clear, it is not always pretty and can certainly be mundane, but the ability to keep doing what needs to be done and putting in the work to get better each time, leads you to the rewards.

Recording expenses this week and not next week gives no insight into your spending habits because the information is flawed, thus making subsequent analyses and decision-making impractical. Similarly, saving money at the beginning of the year only to wastefully spend it all by the end of the summer, does not help you achieve your annual savings goals. Yes, you know *how* to make and save money, but to do so, day in and day out for years to come, is what will get you past the finish line.

The ability to keep going when the targets are not being met and the results are not what was expected, shows determination, and that is achieved by being consistent. Creating that weekly or monthly budget, even though you overspend in a particular category or did not achieve your savings goal, is how you get better at budgeting. You are certainly not going to get better by giving up, only working on the budget when you feel like it, or when you think life is good.

I often hear people say, "Oh, I don't budget because I don't have money to budget," or "I stopped because I wasn't saving any money."

With that laissez-faire attitude, chances are you will never get a better hold on your finances. By failing to continuously put in the work, you will never see where you are going wrong to increase your financial muscle memory. If you do not want to put in the effort because you feel you do not have enough, chances are you will *never* have enough because you only desire the highs of life, and life comes with lows. What is more, if you *do* manage to get enough, sadly you will not have the skills to manage it.

Consistency builds momentum as a result of those repetitive actions. Keeping your head down and plowing on means you will get out of debt, get your sales targets up, and your savings objectives will be achieved. I have a theory that if you keep showing up in the way you need to, at some point, the universe will send a helping hand.

Overnight success does not actually come overnight. It comes after countless hours of putting in work. The reason it may look like overnight, is that no one is paying attention when you are on the Struggle Bus and failing. They only notice when you are achieving and when you explain how much it took to get there. Unfortunately for them, that story is not newsworthy enough, so it is fashioned as an overnight success. Usain Bolt once said, "I trained four years to run nine seconds, and people give up when they don't see results in two months."

Consistency looks like enhancing your development skills, to ensure that you rise to the next level of your career.

Consistency looks like sacrificing materialism to ensure you can fund that development course on your own.

Consistency looks like taking your own lunch to work every day and saving that $3k per year and committing to weekly meal planning to ensure no food wastage.

Consistency looks like making time to schedule regular maintenance on vehicles or appliances.

All these forms of showing up consistently translate financially.

While one (or all) of these activities may not seem beneficial to you, understand that consistent actions towards your financial life can easily translate to a savings of $10k per year. I am sure if someone offered you $10k for no additional work or a little effort, you would eagerly take them up on said offer.

The thing with money is that cents add up to dollars, which then become thousands. And with careful strategy, we get to a million.

FOCUS

"Unless this building is burning down today, I don't want to know about it today."

I have said those words a few times in the work environment, and while coming from a senior manager that may seem harsh or irresponsible to some, the fact is, you must do what needs to be done to create the environment in which you can effectively perform. In a perfect world, I would not need to set those types of boundaries and I am sure practitioners of leadership will have many theories and suggestions; however, we live in an imperfect world, full of distraction, and we are only going to achieve when we learn to focus.

Being laser-focused is the ability to stay in one's lane and smash the goals and targets we set for ourselves, all while the world is crumbling. The world is a distracting place, and the ease of interconnectivity through the World Wide Web has brought many benefits, but it has also decreased our ability to stay focused. Social media's ADHD mannerisms do nothing to help the cause. With its real-time reporting of all sorts of fake news and viral content (which, by the way, adds no value to your long-term objectives), it is way too easy to lose your focus.

Even when you manage to steer yourself clear of the distractions, you must then keep those around you on course as well. Have you ever gotten up in the morning and found some piece of "news" going around? Many times, it is not even in your locale, yet that particular topic seems to be on everyone's lips that day, only for it to be forgotten the next. However, during that twenty-four-hour period, people have spent much of their time consumed by it. That is the type of distraction that keeps you from achieving your goals. To truly stay focused on our objectives, we must create a system which avoids the interferences, so our day is not derailed by whatever headlines are flashing across the screens. It is okay to know what is going on in the world, but if you do not have the ability to stay focused through it all, you are not going to achieve much.

To unlock the next level of financial wealth, you will need to be laser-focused, which will include setting boundaries both with your time and your money. You will be required to treat your time as a financial commodity to ensure you are earning the best return on your assets.

Which will it be? Two hours of aimless scrolling on the Internet, or an hour of scrolling and an hour on your budget forecast? We all have time, but it is how we allocate the time that makes the difference. You can tell yourself you do not have an hour to work on starting a budget because you are working two jobs, when, in fact, you are working two jobs because you have not been able to control your spending because you do not know where your money's going in the first place. The hour you carve out to prioritize these equally important activities, will be the key to unlock your future.

For us to achieve, we must know where we are going. Setting yearly financial goals and targets helps to do that. They can look like saving $10k this year, paying off $25k in loans, or investing $50k in the stock market. Once you have established what those main financial goals are and have broken them down into bite-sized monthly or weekly goals, then your focus comes into play. New Year resolutions and vision boards all appear fancy until May rolls around, and the challenges are upon us. It is then that we realize things are not exactly going the way we expected. Deepening that focus is how you arrive in December, having met that target.

You may get into a fender bender that required expenditure which was certainly *not* in the budget. Circumstances beyond our control may result in the loss of a major client. Daily expenses, such as food and utilities, may be rising at a level far higher than anyone predicted and, in these moments, you are going to have to devise a new game plan. You will have to zero in on how you can still achieve your financial goals. In trying to create solutions for the various challenges that are bound to pop up at some point, you will quickly realise your next best friend in the quality lineup is *adaptability to change*.

ADAPTABILITY TO CHANGE

Being stuck in our ways affects the experiences we have in life, especially when we create a static picture of who we are, where we are going, and how we are going to get there, without leaving room for adaptability. We lose the opportunity to explore other options that may lead to more fulfilling and lucrative results.

Change comes easily for some people and is awfully hard for most, because it requires them to step out of their comfort zone and embrace the unknown. The reason many are afraid of change, is the fear of shifting into a space of not knowing the outcome from the onset, and not having enough knowledge or experience to embrace the change needed.

To fully adapt to change, one must adopt the concept that *all roads lead to home*. If the destination is to provide financially for yourself and your loved ones, then there are many legal and moral avenues which can be pursued that will allow one to reach this objective. Oftentimes, people hold fast to a path that is not working, and instead of tweaking the strategy, they double-down until there is nothing left. This is the reason some successful businesses of yesteryear eventually falter. They fail to adapt their business to the current market.

The best way to embrace the changes needed to advance your financial status, is to understand what portion of your decisions are emotional. Decisions related to money do not need emotions. There are debit and credits, assets, and liabilities - that is it. Once we remove the emotion, the actions we need to take are quite visible. Now, with the emotion out of the equation, you can make the changes necessary to produce the best financial decisions.

Plantain and avocado on your Sunday plate may be what you have known your entire life, but when they are not in season and the price has skyrocketed, is that really the best decision for your supermarket budget? Not when there are other produce in season that are more aligned with it. By removing the emotion of comfort, it becomes easy to see the decision which needs to be made. Practicing with smaller decisions, like your supermarket bill, gives you the confidence to make larger financial changes.

Changes can be made in incremental steps, or they can be approached with a cold-turkey concept. Knowing your personality will determine the best course of action. Incremental changes work best for people who are really stuck and may be crippled by fear but are prepared to try. This method requires an individual to be disciplined and focused on the final task if they are to stay on the course.

The disadvantage with this method, is that those changes may be too small to keep any real momentum, and one difficult day can erode all the wins previously experienced (like how a cheat day turns into a cheat month when you are on a fitness journey).

Cold-turkey works best for motivated persons who possess the mental strength to adopt this method by giving it all they have - no looking back. This method may also be adopted when an individual has tried the incremental approach and become comfortable with the change process and now wants to go all in.

Change Management Techniques

Change requires knowledge of the other options available for you to try, and a decision on how to go about implementing those changes in a way that works for you. It also requires that you unlearn some of what you have been taught. This goes back to the discussion of those traditional behaviours that hinder success. It should be noted, suddenly viewing money or your way of life differently when you have spent decades doing what you were taught, or what you deemed to be best, and implementing the changes needed is not easy. Not only will you encounter the fear of change, but you will also experience the humility of relearning and even disappointment with yourself or those around you, because you will feel you should have known better.

At some point during this journey called 'life', we are going to have a lightbulb moment and think, "How did I not know that?" Once you can go past those feelings, you will have achieved the frame of mind to adapt.

ACCOUNTABILITY

What do you do when you know no one is looking?

During lockdown, I discovered a British television series called Secret Eaters. A camera crew follows people who are confused about why they cannot lose weight. The prevalent theme throughout all the episodes is that there is a stark difference between what people *declared* to have eaten in a day, and what they actually *did* eat. It is both hilarious and mind-boggling.

Holding yourself accountable will be one of the hardest areas of your financial journey.

"I bought three pairs of shoes today because a coworker was rude to me, and I deserved them."

"I don't have time to cook dinner tonight and have to order in because the children are tired and need my attention."

"I didn't hit my revenue numbers because no-one has money to spend."

Or "The phone upgrade didn't cost that much."

These are the lies we tell ourselves and the excuses we allow. The truth is, we bought the shoes because we were unable to process the emotion(s) associated with the feelings which derived from the encounter with the rude person.

Takeout was the solution because of poor planning.

The lack of sales is a result of pursuing a business strategy that is not working, and the phone upgrade was not needed - it was the feeling of having something new and shiny.

When we see through the lies we tell ourselves, we are better able to make sound, financial decisions and hold ourselves accountable. Accountability is hard because it requires us to look in the mirror, not hide, and face awful facts. Digging in and analysing those credit card and bank statements can be a painful exercise. Admitting where you went wrong on the way to being deep in debt can be shocking. To get out of the spiral, you must admit where you are and implement change if you are going to get where you need to be.

Recording your spending daily, analysing weekly, and making the changes necessary to align yourself, is taking steps towards accountability. Finding ways to get back in alignment when you have gone off-track and not allowing one difficult day, week, or month to become final notices on bills, debt collecting agencies, and foreclosures, is accountability.

Accountability is cancelling an outing because the budget was used elsewhere and not throwing a tantrum about it. Accountability requires you to focus on your long-term goals, regardless of what is burning down around you. It requires you to get up every day with the discipline and consistency we spoke about to get through the mundane tasks of life.

Accountability, my friends, is hardcore adulting.

CHAPTER SUMMARY

1. What characteristics listed do you have?
2. Which ones do you need to develop more?
3. Are there any other qualities you would add?

PART II

KNOWLEDGE IS POWER

CHAPTER 6
LIVING ON A BUDGET

Now that we have a general understanding of the life we want to live, how our past influences the financial decisions we make to our good or detriment, and what it takes to live a financially successful life, let us delve into the practicality of how we achieve those things.

Practical Living
Daily Money Habits

We acknowledge that we need money to survive in this world. Regardless of how frugal or lavishly we live, some amount of money is required. We develop good money habits by making them part of our everyday life, not just at the end of the month when the bills are to be paid or at the beginning of the year when we set a budget and never look at it again. Our daily activity must reflect the overall money goal.

An unconventional way to look at your daily money habits, is to theoretically determine how much funds you have from your day's pay when you get home, even before you look at it numerically.

Let's consider an individual who leaves home at 7 AM to drop their child to school and make it to work by 8 AM. They get out the door on time, arrive at the school gate, and give their child $20 for the day. They drive to their parking space, which costs $7 per day, and make it to their desk. About an hour later, they wander to the coffee shop next to their office for breakfast, which costs $15, manage to squeeze in a working lunch for another $15, and an afternoon treat for $5. That's $62 spent before the workday ends.

Hold on, we have not allocated a cost to the smart attire for the day (add another $12 per day), and the student loans to achieve the qualifications to do the job at $32 per day.

Total cost of going to work - $106. Now, this individual may earn $333 per day after taxes, so that seems okay. The problem is, however, they have spent 32% of their earnings simply walking through the office door. This means by the time they receive their monthly salary they only have 68% remaining to cover all their expenses and savings.

This may seem exorbitant in some cases, and this method is not exactly a comprehensive enough picture on which to base financial decisions, but it is a fun way to see how you spend your money and if it aligns with your overall money strategy.

Lunch Money - $20

Parking - $7

Food - $35

Clothing - $12

Student Loans - $32

Total Expenses - $106

BUDGETING 101

Budgeting 101—Living On a Budget

The thought of living life on a budget can be triggering for some. This is because they associate being on a budget with a life of poverty or not ever having enough. Stemming from their childhood upbringing, they may believe that people only live on a budget when they struggle with daily expenses or live pay cheque-to-pay cheque, and that is something they never want to experience again.

For others, their thought process is, "I don't need a budget. I make enough money to take care of me and my family's needs with some to spare." Then there are those who do not even consider budgeting, as they believe that only people who earn large pay cheques need them. In the last few years, I have met each and every one of these people. In the same token, I have met people who budget to the last cent and are successful budgeters.

Not having a budget does not mean an individual will be in financial ruin. Many people have managed to live their adult lives without a budget and not be homeless and, in theory, if you can master the art of not spending more than you earn and saving some for a rainy day, you will be okay financially. However, if 'okay' is not your desired destination, then a budget is your mode of transport.

A budget is a financial plan for how you want to spend money. It is not meant to be a deterrent to living a full life. Rather, its job is to ensure you have the finances to live the life you want and plan for your and your family's future.

Successful businesses are all managed through a budget. This process starts months before the fiscal year commences, and whilst in some cases it can be considered one of the most stressful periods of the financial calendar year, the result lays out the financial map to which the company will follow.

Budget season is no joke. Tempers flare, people's feelings get hurt, deadlines always seem impossible, and regardless of how much you think you have learnt from the last season and all the promises to make the process work better next time, it never happens. Despite this, the ability to precisely know the financial goals and required resources at the beginning of the year, and the joy of smashing those goals, makes it worthwhile.

That budget is a shield for us accountants. It allows us to boldly say, "Sorry, it wasn't in the budget," with a smile. Not that we get pleasure from turning down requests, but it makes people think about the financial consequences of decisions they are making in their departments, and you will learn to do the same with your personal budget.

The same way successful businesses will never go into a new year or month without a budget, then you, as an individual, should not either. Budgeting transforms your financial position. It takes the guesswork out of where you are going to financially finish and allows you to make decisions *now* to achieve the goals you have in mind.

Saving $5k can be achieved without a budget. You may even be able to save $50k with good lifestyle choices; however, saving $1M will take an entirely different strategic approach, which will not be accomplished by bypassing the budgeting process. In theory, you don't *save* $1M—you *achieve* $1M by leveraging your earlier financial accomplishments.

One of the common characteristics of people who live pay cheque to pay cheque and struggle financially, is that they have no idea where their money is going. It is exceedingly difficult to channel your money in the areas you want, if you have no idea what you spend it on in the first place. One of the quickest telltale signs comes when the question is asked, "How much money do you spend on grocery shopping per month?" and when the response is, "I have no idea," that sums up the story.

You know that saying: you break a $100 note, and it disappears. It sure does, but where did it go? Actively logging your expenses can be a real revelation. Those little trips for an afternoon snack add up. The frequent trips to the supermarket without a list turn into a massive number every month, and the eating-out number is a slap in the face. Sure, we all must eat, but are you prepared to work hard just to be able to buy food?

As a newbie budgeter, the first step (for which you do *not* need any financial knowledge) is to start logging your expenses. This process can start even before you begin to work with a budget, as a budget is only as good as the data you use. This is the information you will need for that process.

By logging expenses, and experiencing the initial shock of how one spends their money, the process will reveal that, based on the monthly outgoings, there is not enough revenue coming in. This can be a hidden factor for a long time because of the refusal to create a working budget and/or from not properly recording expenses. The only way you can work on a solution to a problem, is first by being able to identify what the problem is, and the budgeting process will show you when there is a revenue gap.

While a solution is being worked on to increase revenue, in the interim, a cutback in expenses can immediately be put in place. Again, this is achievable if you have an idea of how your monies are being spent.

DATE	DETAILS	CATEGORY	TOTAL
TOTAL			**$**

"I have a lot of debt, so I don't have a budget because there is no money to budget."

That is exactly *why* you need a budget. If you are paying down substantial amounts of debt without a plan, you are resorting to being in that debt for however long. To free yourself from debt, you must be committed to repay it within the smallest amount of time. To do that, you will need to make payments greater than the minimum and have a strategic plan for how you want to attack it - and in what order. To be able to allocate additional funds to the debt, you must be able to see where the funds are going to come from, and determine what the best strategy would be for your circumstance. Throwing all your extra money at substantial debt without an emergency fund, will still leave you in a vulnerable financial position, and the ability to make sound financial decisions can only be met if you have a financial plan - aka, a budget.

For example, you are driving down the street, land in a pothole and burst a tire. Without an emergency fund and no help from the insurance company, that new tire will most likely be paid for via credit card. In theory, you are taking one step forward and two steps backward, hence why it is recommended you establish an emergency fund as part of your 'get-out-of-debt' strategy.

The emotion associated with having a new car, the vacation of a lifetime or a comfortable sleep in your own home - choose one. There are some who can afford all at the same time and many who *think* they can. Mapping out a financial plan will show you which category you fall into and allow you to make responsible decisions.

Budgeting is not restrictive. It helps you make decisions that lead you to living the life you desire. By having this map before you, the ability to prioritise the areas of your life that are most important becomes more profound. Frequent trips to the salon, bars, and weekly brunch sessions may feel like just what you need, and entertainment should be a healthy part of our lives, but are you prepared to still be paying for these expenses six months to a year later because you used debt to purchase them? Are you willing to never take a family holiday, or not ever be able to retire because you are drowning in debt?

The thought of creating a budget seems daunting to some non-financial persons, and there is a misconception that you must acquire a sea of financial knowledge to begin. However, a simple budget can be drafted on a napkin - it is that easy. Budgeting is one of those skills that improves the more you practice. As your proficiency improves, you move to higher levels, but, as with all things, getting started is the hard part.

As a newbie budgeter, you start with a budget based on your pay period, that is, weekly, bi-weekly or monthly. Then record your incoming revenue. I suggest using your net pay (after taxes have been deducted). There is no point in looking at the gross amount if you have no choice about the compulsory taxes taken from your remuneration.

If your remuneration is not a set amount per period or is commission-based, I suggest you look at your revenue in the last year and use that. Make any adjustments, as needed, especially if in the prior year there was a circumstance that is not relevant to the current period (such as a major job that has finished). In such a case, adjust accordingly. For example, you can reduce the revenue by a percentage. Let's say the contribution of that job to the overall revenue was 15%, then that would be a good starting point. Bank statements or a call to your company's payroll department will help you get the ball rolling.

Next, move onto your expected expenses. Again, the best source of information comes from past spending, as outlined in your banking statements and from the data you have collected by recording your expenses. For this portion, you will also need to know those expenses which are not part of your daily living but are paid bi-annually or yearly (such as car insurance, vacation, house maintenance, and special occasions). Factor them into your budget.

As you move on from the basic level of budgeting to a more intermediate level, sinking funds will become part of your budgeting process as well. *Sinking funds* are buckets of money set aside for future expenses. They can be either short-term (e.g., birthdays, electronics, or house repairs) or geared towards longer financial goals (e.g., a down payment for a home or tuition). Having visibility on these categories allows you to work on funding these expenses at every pay period, which then allows the required monies to be there when the expenses become due. They also avoid a situation in which you find yourself needing to find 'X' dollars within a short period of time, thus resorting to funding that expense through debt (this is how credit card debt spirals).

Emergency funds will be your next level of defence in your financial journey. As outlined in an upcoming section entitled *Save, Save, and Save some more*, they are there to protect you, to keep you going when life's moments happen or should you lose your income. An emergency fund can be built in the same manner as sinking funds, little by little, and based on the events of the last two-plus years, it may be apparent to some people that the level of funds they previously had will not be enough for the current world we live in.

The final part of the budgeting process involves the distribution of the remaining money after all expenses are paid, and allocations made to the sinking funds. Those remaining monies are your disposable income, and it unlocks the key to your future life. After all, we did not come to earth only to pay bills and die. Your disposable income will allow you to build the life and live the lifestyle you desire.

Most importantly, the budget must balance. That is, the expenses must not be more than the revenue. The only budgets that consistently do not balance are the government ones. Everyone else will need a balanced budget. If you have prepared a budget that does not balance, then it is a clear indication that there is an urgent matter that needs to be addressed, because the only way to proceed will require you to take on debt.

That is not a preferred option.

At advanced levels of budgeting, a zero net budget is effective. This style of budgeting allocates every dollar to a category, whether expenses, savings, or investments. This process helps you to openly see how much is being distributed to investing activities and can be broken down by accounts for easy tracking (e.g., saving accounts, investment accounts, term deposits, real estate). At this level, the budget allocation becomes more visual.

MONEY IN	BUDGET	ACTUAL
EARNINGS		
ADDITIONAL INCOME		
TOTAL INCOME		

MONEY OUT	BUDGET	ACTUAL
AUTOMOBILE (GAS, INSURANCE, TAXES, REPAIRS)		
BANK CHARGES (FEES, CC ANNUAL FEE)		
BILLS (CELLPHONE, CABLE)		
CLOTHING		
CHILDREN (CLOTHING, SCHOOL FEES, SPORTS)		
DINING & ENTERTAINMENT		
GROCERIES		
HEALTHCARE (INSURANCE, DOC VISITS)		
HOBBIES (SPORTS, BOOKS, GYM)		
HOUSING (RENT, MORTGAGE, TAXES, INSURANCE)		
MISCELLANEOUS (EMERGENCY FUND)		
PERSONAL CARE (TOILETRIES, COSMETICS, SPA)		
TAXES		
TRAVEL & HOTEL LODGING		
UTILITIES (ELEC, GAS, PHONE, GAS, INTERNET)		
LOANS (STUDENT, MEDICAL)		
TOTAL EXPENSES		

SINKING FUNDS	BUDGET	ACTUAL
HOUSE REPAIRS		
BIRTHDAYS		
CHRISTMAS		
TRAVEL		
CAR		
MAINTENANCE		
EVENTS		
BIRTHDAYS		

SAVINGS	BUDGET	ACTUAL
SAVINGS ACCOUNT		
RETIREMENT ACCOUNT		
INVESTMENTS		
TOTAL SAVINGS		

MONEY LEFT OVER	BUDGET	ACTUAL

BUDGET ALLOCATIONS

Budget percentage allocations are important in meeting your financial goals, regardless of whether you are a basic budgeter or at the advanced level. Additionally, they should be customised per an individual's goals and their age.

The 50/30/20 rule was made popular by US Senator Elizabeth Warren. The theory suggests that no more than 50% of your income should go towards living expenses, 30% towards wants and 20% towards saving. As a starting point, this is a simplistic way to allocate your income to ensure you are working towards your goals and, most importantly, that you are contributing towards your savings.

To create a financial plan that works for your individual needs, you will be required to make accommodations and some deviations from the standard rules. Following the usual path might get you there, but if you want to go beyond the usual path, then you need to divert from the usual ways. By following the standard path between living expenses and wants, 80% of your income is being spent on expenses that do not produce a return. That is based on the premise that the living expenses do not include any amounts being allocated to a real estate asset, or that the portion is minimal.

For a young person who has started working and is at a stage where they want to enjoy a bit of life before the real financial obligations come, *if* that individual does not have excessive student loans which need attention, the standard allocation will serve them. As a person gets older with a family and other obligations and goals, only putting aside 20% will not be enough for savings and investing, thanks to the current world economy and the uncertainty that appears every ten-to-twelve years, due to extraordinary events.

For persons who are desirous of building a career that involves various levels of development to reach the pinnacle, they will need to allocate a portion of income to their personal development from an early stage (as discussed further in a later chapter). The onus is on you to ensure you allocate the resources to take your career to the next level. Individuals at the foundation level of their career should consider setting aside up to 5% for this purpose. Once spent strategically, this investment will result in an increase in that person's earning capacity. This allocation category can also be used as seeding funds to create a business or a new stream of income.

The savings allocations can be customised based on what an individual is trying to achieve. An upcoming section entitled *Saving Money With Zeros and Commas* highlights how one can reach their goals, whether they are retiring early or increasing their overall wealth by funding their savings allocations.

With those adjustments, the Fun Category allocation will be reduced, and at some point along the financial journey, the reality is, unless you have inherited unlimited amounts of cash, the priorities of building a successful financial life will take precedence over fun. There is a season for everything under the sun. If you stay focused and make the necessary sacrifices during the building season, the play season will be more rewarding.

Budgeting should not be seen as a one-size-fits-all or static document. Rather, it should be adapted as many times as life demands. As an individual gets older and embarks on various life adventures, allocations will be adjusted, categories will be added and removed, and this is expected. For example, as an individual increases their income, it would be expected that the 50% Living Expenses category will start to decrease, shifting to an allocation with more disposable income.

BUDGETING MISTAKES

If you've tried budgeting and have given up or were left completely frustrated, there may be a few reasons why. Two of the most common errors include the fact that estimating irregular income can be difficult. As mentioned earlier, a starting point would be to use prior period income information and adjust based on the current situation. If income fluctuates from period to period, it's important to pay special attention to revenue being earned to ensure you're not overestimating revenue. This will lead to overspending. With fluctuating revenue, it's always best to only spend on basic expenses and delay other spending when the income to do so has been secured.

Another mistake comes from missing expenses, especially the one-off expenses which can sometimes be forgotten until it is time to pay them. Having those sinking funds helps eliminate this issue, but of course, you need to remember these expenses to include them in the Sinking Funds category in the first place. This is where organisation comes in. Successfully managing your financial life *does* involve being organised (aka, adulting).

Some of the most forgotten budget categories stem around events that require expenditure but aren't often considered in the budgeting process. These include birthdays, Valentine's Day, anniversaries, etc., as well as financial gifts. (Whether these amounts were intended to be gifts or loans is another matter, because we all know that most times, the chance of these amounts being repaid is slim.) If you're going to consistently do this, it's better to include a category in your budget as opposed to having your financial goals be sabotaged. This way, you're actively deciding how much you *can* afford and have a better chance of avoiding what you *can't* afford to lose.

Managing The Budget

Creating a master budget to manage your financial life is the first part of the budgeting process. Your success, however, will be determined by your ability to manage that budget. Managing your budget is a daily task but one that should be done in a simple format to avoid it becoming another full-scale item on the to-do list.

The options available for creating and managing your budget can be paper-based, electronic (using a spreadsheet), the envelope system, or an app. Having a system to keep track of your daily expenses will determine how successful you are at maintaining your budget; and while using cash is the best way to keep persons who struggle with spending limits accountable, it is also harder to keep track of.

Good budgeting habits to develop, include periodically checking back in with your budget, and not just setting and forgetting it until it is time for the major review. As time goes by, living on a budget will become second nature and you will instinctively know your financial limits and be able to stay within its confines. When you become one with your budget, your weekly, bi-weekly, or monthly supermarket bill will not be cause for alarm.

For me, as a seasoned budgeter, my fascination with budgeting is the ability to enhance any budget regardless of how good the initial one was. Improving your budget through the intermediate and advanced level, will see you working with one which is similar to what companies produce. At this level, this experience can be transferred to a side business or hustle with an aim to improve financial results.

Identifying fixed and variable costs in your budget and being able to separate expenses into these categories, offers additional benefits. This is an exercise which is vital when cutting expenses, as understanding the correlation between each of these categories and the bottom line is crucial.

At the more advanced level, creating a twelve-month budget brings additional benefits, as it enables you to incorporate cash flows in the process and re-forecast monthly. Now, these are not skills that will impact the ability to live a sound financial life, but when utilised, will take your budget to the level on par with that of multi-million-dollar companies. They take any guesswork out of your financial results at the end of the year and make it much easier to see which parts of the budget need additional assistance (Read: which parts of your *life* need assistance).

At this level, you can manage your overall net worth and go to another one. If your objective is to retire early, be a millionaire, or build generational wealth, managing your net worth is the track to be on.

Budgeting can be as complicated or as simple as you want it to be. The skills are easy to increase as time goes by and can easily be transferred to the business environment, whether it is your own or the one you work for. Regardless of your occupation, any senior level position will require some level of budgeting skills, and managers who are able to gain increased performance in their departments, are those who have some level of budgeting skills and understand the drivers behind their allocations.

FRUGAL LIVING

It is no secret that the key to financial wealth and security is frugal living. This theory is not new and has been written about for decades. In fact, it is the crux of the book, "The Millionaire Next Door," by Thomas J. Stanley.

The term is not a new concept as much as it is a new terminology. Frugal living was common up until the late '90s when credit became widely available.

The lifestyle which most of us over a certain age are accustomed to, is the art of frugal living. That is, being mindful of how you spend your money, which means utilising all resources and options before deciding to part ways with it. When we did purchase something new, we saved and selected the best option available because we wanted it to last a lifetime. Our clothes were mended, and our cars and equipment were repaired as many times as feasible. We cooked and ate what we had, did not run off to the supermarket for one item and came come back with fifteen, grew vegetables and raised the livestock we could with whatever space we had. Our items lasted us a long time, too. Remember when washing machines lasted for twenty or more years? They certainly do not make them that way anymore.

Done correctly, frugal living allows you to keep your money and enjoy the benefits of it for as long as possible, with the ability to create wealth that can be passed onto the next generation. It gives you the comfort of knowing that when life happens (as it will at some point), you will most likely be able to weather the storm.

During the pandemic, if there was one financial lesson that people learnt, it was that frugal living was the way to go. Not only has the pandemic stolen jobs and livelihoods, but with the increase in prices and shrinkflation, the uncertainty of the future has created the need for budget adjustments.

Frugal living is not about living cheaply or having a deprived life, but more about getting the most out of your money. The objective is to maximise your spending power and enjoy the fruits of your labour. This can be achieved by not paying full price for items, not buying inferior products, not spending money on things you do not need, living an authentic life and, most of all, living within your means.

Frugal living may look like taking lunch to work, driving a car that is paid for, learning a skill that saves you money, buying quality over quantity and overall, getting the best bang for your buck. It will involve the dissecting of expenses and categorising them as either fixed or variable. It will also involve analysing each category of expense to determine if every dollar is being spent in the best way. In simple terms, you will need to separate your *needs* from your *wants*.

Let's add to the chart.

REVENUE – EXPENSES = SAVINGS

EXPENSES = FIXED COST +VARIABLE COST

Fixed Cost vs Variable Cost

The aim of this exercise is to understand how much of your revenue goes to those fixed living expenses (the ones which remain the same each month with little or no allowance for change), and how much is left. The portion which remains is the key to the life and future you are carving out for yourself. This is also known as *residual income.*

By completing this exercise, you will be able to calculate the portion of your disposable income that goes to your fixed/living expenses and the portion that remains and goes to your savings, investing, and other expenses. The lower your fixed expenses allocation is, the more choices and flexibility you will have.

From the simple example below, you will see 47% of the income relates to housing with a further 14% on loans, for a total of 61% in fixed cost and 5% to savings. Using the example, we can see that 61% of the income is spent on expenses that must be paid every month.

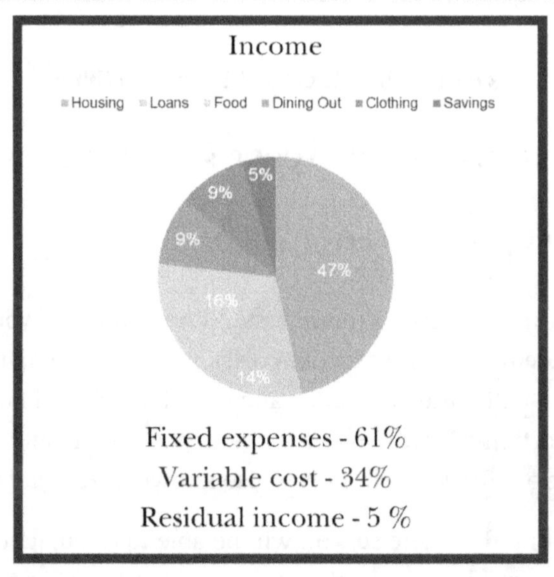

Frugal living means living for less. Having funds readily available gives you options, which translates into your ability to save even more money. Being able to save on big purchases is one of the most critical money-moves, as it relates to frugal living. Whether a piece of land, a vehicle, furniture or travel, frugal persons will try *not* to pay full price, and the first step to being able to do that, is by having disposable income available to catch the market. In frugality, cash is king.

Research is the favourite pastime of frugalist persons. They know impulse-buying is not an option, and to get the best price for the best quality product at the right time, they must know the product they are after. They spend a fair amount of time researching any item or large purchase they intend to make. They will know the best timing to buy or determine the best price, and with financial resources readily available, they will bait time until the market conditions are best suited for that purchase.

Research goes further than just the initial price. A savvy financial person will also ensure they research the maintenance cost, taxes, covenants, and all the fine print that comes with purchases. Often, people make purchases without getting into the details only to realise they did not factor in related expenses. If only they had done so in the beginning, their choice may have looked different. Fine print is where the demons live. That is why advertisers make certain you need a magnifying glass to read it properly.

The common theme of living a financially responsible life, is *living within one's means.* If you follow the rules of frugal living, you will be able to master this. To do this, you must stay true to your budget. Unless it is a matter of life and death, if it is not in the budget, then you cannot afford it. Not being able to afford something does not make you less of a person, nor does it signal poverty. It simply means at that point in time, your priorities do not allow you to spend money on a particular item. If you want to live a financially fruitful life, you need to get comfortable telling yourself (and maybe others), "At this point in time, I can't afford it." There is no logic to going on a holiday or purchasing a material item and having to finance it for the next two years with credit card payments.

Someone may have grown up with a nice car or cable television and not have realised that these items are luxuries. Therefore, they are under the impression that such items form part of the regular living expenses. Taking this thought even further, an individual who has enjoyed the privilege of going to private school or taking part in extracurricular activities will want the same for their offspring because it is considered to be their standard of living.

The truth is, that was their *parents'* standard of living, and unless they have been blessed with a trust fund, if they plan to continue in that way, they must now earn it.

This becomes extremely stressful and confusing for some and is a factor in why people struggle to live within their means. At every point of your financial journey, you must be willing to *act your wage.*

Regardless of what your standard of living was at any point in your life, you must accept where you are at the current point in time and work your way towards the life you desire.

Adopting a frugal lifestyle is a practice that, once perfected, will truly serve its purpose as your income grows. If you cannot manage $5, you will not be able to manage $5,000. This is why statistics show that 70% of persons who win the lottery go broke in five years or less. If you have not mastered the art of living within your means and managing your money as your revenue increases, your expenses will skyrocket, and you will be no better off than those lottery winners. This is known as *lifestyle inflation* or *lifestyle creep and* is usually a result of not dealing with the emotion surrounding money decisions.

Understanding why you spend your money in the way you do is very important. Overspending is not only a result of not being able to manage money, but is also a consequence of underlying emotions. It is very possible to have a substantial amount of revenue and still live pay cheque to pay cheque and have no savings (or a net worth that is below the average for your income bracket). It matters not how much you earn, but how much you can keep.

SAVE, SAVE, AND SAVE SOME MORE

Growing up I heard adults ask what a particular person planned to do with all their money, and if they were trying to buy an airplane. This is one of the common ignorant comments that has been floating around our communities for generations as it relates to money. Looking back, what was considered a lot of money was really an individual with a steady income who most likely had an additional source.

These types of comments are usually in communities where the daily struggle is seen as a normal part of life, where financial knowledge is very lacking and anyone who appears to be earning a decent income and not spending frivolously is deemed peculiar.

To answer that question, maybe the individual *is* desirous of buying an airplane - and nothing is wrong with that. Then there are people who see saving as an activity only designated for a particular purpose, such as a down payment for a house, education, vacation, or to buy an expensive item. The concept of saving for saving's sake or for a rainy day is not part of their financial plan. This may actually seem foreign to many of us who have always been told to save for a rainy day, such as an unexpected expense, the loss of a job, or an unwelcome sickness.

With the more complicated world we live in, saving for a rainy day is not enough. We must be more intentional with our money to ensure we have the amount required to navigate through the pits of life. The occurrences of the last few years, while not anything we could ever have predicted, show that a rainy day can turn into a rainy year; and while it may seem nobody could have prepared for such events, the reality is that those living a responsible financial life have a better chance of weathering the storms.

The first level of defence for a financial setback should be our **emergency fund**. That fund is there for when a life situation pops up unexpectedly. This can be from anything from roof damage sustained during a hurricane (which is not covered by insurance) to a small medical emergency. Of course, there are larger emergencies, like losing your job - and yes, this emergency fund should be there to steady that blow. Based on the above scenarios and how they go from one extreme to the next, it should be enough to tell you there is a need to have a substantial amount available.

In the worst-case scenario, an emergency fund should be able to maintain you until you have secured another source of income. Therefore, to calculate how much emergency fund you need, it must (like all financial decisions) be specific to you.

If you are in a field where your expertise is in demand, the jobs in your field are plentiful, or you have skills that are interchangeable and can easily be utilised, the size of your emergency fund will be smaller than an individual who is in a saturated field or one where jobs are dwindling.

The next factor to consider is what your **bare-bones budget** looks like. That is a budget with just the basic living expenses needed to survive and stay current with financial obligations. In the event of losing your income, the first decision should be to tighten your belt and release the luxury and non-essential items.

Bare Bones

Housing
Food
Utilities
Insurance
Personal care (incl. medication)

Barebones Budget per month * estimate time it takes to find a job
= Emergency Fund

That may seem excessive in some regards, but that is the world we live in. It is time for our financial behaviours to match it.

Depending on the size of the fund, you will want to ensure you are making sound decisions as it relates to risk and liquidity. It is possible that you may never need it. There is also the possibility you may need to access it urgently and will want to do so without large penalties.

The budgeting exercise tells you how much of your disposable income you can save or channel to investing activities. This is why it is vital to a successful financial life. Without that budgeting process, you can get frustrated thinking you are unable to save when, the fact is, you do not have a full picture of your expenses. As a result, you will be unaware of what your savings possibilities are to begin with.

Once you see the full picture laid out before you, you will have the information needed to make the changes to hit your savings goals.

Saving Money With Zeros and Commas

Being able to save every pay period is a sure and steady way to reach your financial goals; however, an accelerated savings plan may look more attractive to you. For persons who want to save money with zeros and commas, a desire of those who are after financial independence within a specific time, or the FIRE brigade (Financial Independence, Retire Early), this route may be more attractive. Financial independence means a person has the ability to support themselves financially without the need to rely on a traditional source of income, or anyone else, for the remainder of their life.

This type of lifestyle is becoming increasingly attractive. Once seen as something only achievable by 1% of the population, it is now achievable for the average person who wants to live differently than what societal norms dictate.

Whether you want to retire early or not, retirement should also be on every working adult's mind. In the current economic environment, with the aging population and the borrowings of many governments from the social security funds, the retirement age in most countries is on the rise. What was once sixty-five years old for retirement, has now increased to seventy years old in some countries, and there are people who currently do not see being able to retire as an option at all. Add that to the current stress levels within working environments, and it is no wonder many are breaking traditions and looking for balance.

Those who want to break traditional money habits and not leave their financial life to chance, are more willing to adopt a laser-focused approach to savings. Before one embarks on such a journey, they should ensure they have mastered the budgeting process, funded an emergency fund, paid debt down to zero or the lowest possible manageable balance and, most importantly, have a consistent source of income.

Once these matters are settled, then the process of saving money with commas and zeros can commence. To quantify this as a savings percentage, an accelerated savings plan could be a rate of between 30% and 75% as an annual amount. This laser-focused approach entails working with your bare-bones budget and sending all your surplus income to the bottom line. This is not an easy task and even the most focused individuals will find it difficult to live like this for a prolonged period, which is why one must take a realistic approach to this lifestyle.

A more realistic approach to this method to ensure success would be to pursue bare-bones living for three to six months (to establish consistency) and then re-add the items which were cut from the budget that are needed for a more mentally sustainable lifestyle. For example, if you completely cut dining out from your budget but as a result are physically exhausted or no longer have time to spend with your family, then you will need to revisit that expense to bring balance back to your life. The idea is *not* to burn out, but to make enough changes for you to see a substantial shift in your net worth in as little time as possible.

This approach can be used by those who may feel as if they are late to the savings and investing game. By employing the same approach, it is possible to establish a saving pattern that gives you the motivation for saving, thus making it a natural part of your financial journey.

To add gravy to this dish, seek to increase your revenue whilst maintaining your same lifestyle. Do not fall prey to lifestyle creeps and you will see 100% flow through of that extra income.

That is where the secret lies.

If you can continuously do this through successive pay increases (not inflation adjustments), then financial independence can be well within your grasp.

I first started to look at this bare-bones approach shortly after returning from my travel sabbatical. At the time, I was unaware that it had a name. My objective was to keep my costs as low as possible, while I transitioned from the travel life back to that of the working masses. Living on a travel budget was financially freeing, as the objective of the budget was to spend it, not preserve it. Now back in the real world, I analysed all my expenses in a thorough way, digging deep into the supermarket bills, etc.

Once I had returned to full-time employment, I continued to hold my budget tight and that brought a new perspective on what I could achieve. Over the years, I have intentionally reset my lifestyle and budget to keep myself in check, because no one spends more money than a person who knows where their next pay cheque is coming from. A consistent and reliable pay cheque is a good thing, but it can also make you complacent with one too many lifestyle creeps.

CHAPTER 7
DEBT MANAGEMENT

Prior to the introduction of widespread credit, it was difficult for black Caribbean working-class people to secure credit, as they were mostly financially excluded by the banking system. There are a few published studies on this topic which look at the history of the banks in the Caribbean and the connection to racial capitalism.

There is no doubt that this era of debt introduction resulted in growth for economies and individuals and allowed the working-class to get on the property ladder and propel their financial lives; however, it came at a cost. Fast forward to the introduction of 100% mortgages and easy cash and credit from various sources at ridiculous rates, and the debt levels have continued to increase to unbelievable amounts, with no slowing down in sight.

With the inevitable recession following the pandemic, one must wonder, will the debt crisis ever wane? For starters, the average household currently carries way more debt than it should. Add this to the additional amounts being racked up by various governments, and it all looks very bleak for the generations to come.

In the current environment, there are many types of debt an individual can carry, such as mortgages, student loans, medical bills, credit cards, payday loans, small business loans, vehicle loans, hire purchases, store cards and personal loans such as vehicle, travel, back to school, and Christmas loans. Each type of debt will carry features that are unique to the agreement and to the borrower. Shockingly, many people enter into these agreements every day without truly understanding what they are signing on to.

GOOD DEBT VERSUS BAD DEBT

Debt, in and of itself, is not a bad thing. The challenge of debt comes with the level and type you are carrying. Debt can be categorised as good or bad based on its characteristics. *Good debt* will increase your overall net worth in the foreseeable future or is attached to an asset that appreciates.

Mortgage debt, generally the highest debt individuals carry, is considered good, since it is attached to an asset that can be considered an appreciating asset. For many, this is most of their net worth, and their financial future is directly attached to this asset. Student loans are other forms of debt that can be considered good debt, as the outlay is expected to produce a return of future revenue and income. Business loans can also fall into the category of good debt based on the future returns of the investment.

Like everything in life, good debt needs a disclaimer. Not *all* mortgages, student or business loans are good debt, and unfortunately, many only realise this when their financial life is in tatters. The sad reality is that some are carrying mortgages above what they can actively manage, while still maintaining other money obligations with whatever money is left over; or they are taking on mortgages which require double income for the household to manage and those which are secured at the height of the market, which end up under water in times of recession.

Underwater mortgages are those in which the current market value of the property is less than the outstanding balance.

The other major factor which contributes to whether a mortgage is a good debt, is the fact that most individuals view their investment as a dwelling for the purpose of *living* and not as an *investment*. By doing so, they make decisions based on emotions that do not see the asset being kept in a saleable condition. Your pink kitchen cabinets may be what you have always dreamed of, but if you decide to sell the house, those cabinets will need to be repainted to give you the best chance to capitalise on your investment.

Just as mortgages are not always good debt, the same applies to student loans. After a mortgage, this is the next biggest level of debt, and the trend is worrying. Student loan debt is the ball and chain of the millennial generation, whereas mortgages were that of their parents.

In a quest for further personal development or for an advantage over the market, many are entering into high levels of student loan debt. Theoretically, this should yield a return on investment that justifies the expense. Unfortunately, we are in an era where some of these qualifications are not worth the paper they are printed on, as higher education has now become just another big business.

Before embarking on such a journey, people need to be honest with themselves. One must consider the ultimate earning capacity of the profession they are pursuing, for how many years they are going to be on the hook for the outlay, and whether the investment will allow for the career progression they are after *before* they agree to sign on the dotted line. Most importantly, they need to be certain they are sure that is the academic and professional path they want to follow. It is quite disheartening to be paying a student loan for a qualification you have not used and have no intention of using.

Bad debts are those which are attached to assets that depreciate in time, or for lifestyle expenses that have no return on the outlay, or those that carry excessive levels of fees. Most types of debt fall into this category and despite knowing this, the trend continues because they are packaged and marketed so beautifully. They appeal to instant gratification in an era where we want it all and we want it now.

To be clear, even manageable levels of bad debt will not ruin an individual's financial position. That happens when said individual becomes deep in debt. The difference between being *in debt* and *deep in debt* occurs when the individual is unable to service the debt when it becomes due, or when their debt ratio calculation exceeds acceptable levels. Persons end up here when they lack the financial knowledge needed to effectively manage their lives, or when they believe they can manipulate the system; and as the saying goes, "The house always wins."

To qualify for a loan with traditional financial institutions, your debt-to-income ratio will be calculated. If a person has reached the acceptable limit (the limit that allows a borrower to meet their obligations and still maintain a healthy financial life) they will be turned down.

How people get themselves into the deep end, is by choosing to find other avenues to continue borrowing above the acceptable level, and this is where mezzanine type debt comes into play. This type of financing carries a higher interest ratio and is mostly accessed via credit cards, payday loans, or loans via non-financial institutions.

CREDIT CARD DEBT

The third highest level of household debt in Barbados stems from credit cards. According to the Central Bank of Barbados, by the end of March 2020, credit card debt totalled BDS$295 million - a 220% increase in just twenty years. Credit cards became popular among the general population in the late '90s, and whilst many welcome the latest version of debt, just as many people initially shun it out of fear of getting into debt because of lack of knowledge.

Today, there continues to be a minority of persons who still do not have or have never owned a credit card for these reasons. However, for the most part, most adults use credit cards as part of their normal financial lives. These individuals fall into two categories: those who have the knowledge to use them responsibly and those who do not.

Used responsibly, there are benefits to regular use of credit cards. The initial attraction was the ease of making payments. Prior to having access to a credit card, making international purchases meant going into a commercial bank and waiting in line to secure a banker's draft, then sending said draft via the post office or courier. That method took time. Credit card transactions took care of that lengthy and more costly process. That transaction also involved the individual having monies readily available to secure the draft, as bankers' drafts must be paid for in advance.

Fast forward to the current day. In addition to the convenience, the added perks of having a credit card include cashback, airplane miles, travel insurance coverage, store points, and exclusive deals and entertainment packages for cardholders. Many credit card issuers will even try to lure new users by offering a lump sum of miles or no interest on transferred balances - the gimmicks are endless.

In this era, no responsible credit cardholder should be using a card which does not offer them additional benefits. Furthermore, they should take time to secure the card that works best for them and their lifestyles.

For travellers, the attraction of airplane miles is a major perk, as cardholders can obtain free flights using miles acquired from daily spending expenses. However, most card issuers will require the taxes on those tickets to be paid. Once the card balance is paid in full when due, you will incur no interest or added cost.

Others prefer cards that give them a cash rebate based on a percentage of the monies they have spent and will have this rebate factored into their yearly budgets, or they will decide what expense they want to put that rebate against.

Of course, not all cardholders use their cards responsibly, hence why credit card debt has become such a major factor for most. There are a few reasons why. Most credit card debt holders admit to not having full knowledge of how credit cards work, before they assumed the risk of using the card. This might include not understanding how cut-off dates work, the excessive interest rates and how they are applied, and the disadvantages of cash withdrawals.

Cash withdrawals from credit cards should be the *last* resort for any cardholder, and should only be justified in the case of dire emergencies. This is because they incur interest from the moment the transaction takes place and not when the balance becomes due, as is the case with other purchases made using the card. In some cases, cash advances also carry an interest rate that is higher than the original interest rate of the card and there will be a transaction fee, usually a percentage of the amount of that cash advance.

The point at which the devil is in the details regarding cash advances, is their repayment. Unless the balance is paid in full, there is no guarantee that you are paying the original interest, and not the one associated with the advance. Most credit card companies will put payments to the oldest balances first and will not treat the cash advance separately. This is usually buried in the fine print, which, unfortunately, is not typically read by applicants or not understood.

Notwithstanding the lack of knowledge of how credit cards work, the stark reality is that individuals deem credit cards to be using the *bank's* money. Some people do not understand that, with each swipe of that card, the transaction is actually a *loan* from the bank to them, and as with all loans, it will need to be repaid in due course.

The larger pitfall of how individuals use credit cards stems from the repayment of these balances when they become due. The minimum rate, as outlined by the statement, should be considered a *suggestion*. For example, a balance of $1,000 at an interest rate of 21%, with a minimum payment of 1% of the outstanding balance plus interest, will take approximately twenty-six months (about two years) to clear —and that is with the assumption that payments cannot be less than $20, if there are no other purchases made to the card.

Chances are, there will be more purchases made and the credit card use will become a revolving credit. While this works great for financial institutions, it creates dependence for the cardholder. Such a dependency becomes more prevalent when the cardholders do not have a working budget or lack necessary budgeting skills.

A common mistake in budgeting, is to input the total of the credit card payment paid in that period. As a result, individuals are fooled into believing they are within their budgets because they can afford the payment, which may be the minimum. By doing this, the budget shortfall is not visual, and people do not realise they are supplementing their income shortfall using credit. In theory, every month that this happens, you are taking out a loan (however small) to meet your monthly obligations.

Not everyone with credit card debt lacks knowledge. Some are simply using it as a temporary measure to hold them over or to see them out of a bleak period, having few options at the time, with little to no income coming in.

To become a responsible cardholder, one must address the underlying issues which caused them to become in debt via credit cards. In this way, they can begin to end the cycle. Without this phase, persons have the tendency to consolidate credit card debt to a personal loan with a lower interest rate, and then simply carry on swiping the credit card, thereby plunging themselves further into debt and limiting their credit options for the future.

PAYDAY LOANS

At some point on the journey to being deep in debt, payday loans come into the equation, usually when the individual has exhausted all other sources of traditional credit because their debt-to-income ratio has now increased to an unsustainable amount and the traditional sources of debt have turned them away. Payday loans are mezzanine type funding. That is, they are unsecured and serve to bridge the gap. This is reflected in their high interest rates. This type of debt was originally there to help one get from one pay cheque to another, by allowing them to borrow tiny amounts of money, which they would repay with their next pay cheque; however, the current tactics of payday loan companies are predatory in nature. They reel people in with quick and easy processing, and once seen as a tie-over from one payday to the next, the amounts one can access have drastically increased.

Moreover, they are able to secure repayment through employment deductions, thereby reducing the risk to the company but leaving many workers without a sustainable net wage on which to survive. In my opinion, these companies should be considered legal loan sharks.

GETTING OUT OF DEEP DEBT

Getting out of deep debt takes a lot of commitment, a mindset shift, and tough decisions. Extreme effort to get out of debt may involve selling your home, car, and other possessions. Another option might include taking on additional employment to reduce it to a manageable amount or be rid of it altogether.

If you are deep in debt and do not have the financial knowledge to get yourself out, or feel overwhelmed, anxious or depressed over your financial situation, you should seek professional advice. Strategies for getting out of debt should not only be geared towards your unique situation, but also be tailored to your environment.

Financial rules and regulations are not interchangeable and the bankruptcy laws which exist in some countries do not in others. You can do more harm to yourself if you are working with information that is not geared to your jurisdiction.

Before deciding on what strategy works for you, one thing you need to know is how much debt you are actually in.

When are those monies due?

What are the interest rates?

Are any overdue? Have any been sent to a debt collection agency or have legal proceedings been started?

You will need to know the answers to those questions.

Next, if you are not currently servicing any of the debts, contact the creditors and openly communicate your current situation. Hiding or pretending the debt is not there will make it worse. Creditors will not be able to make suggestions or assist if you do not communicate with them, but with some conversation, they may be able to reduce the monthly payment or offer some other solution for a temporary reprieve.

Create a monthly debt schedule which comprises all the debt obligations and pairs them against your disposable income (see Appendix).

When deciding on a strategy to allocate the disposable funds you have available, you can include a combination of the following:

1. Pay the minimum on all amounts to avoid late fees and finance charges.
2. Consolidate debts with higher interest rates (e.g., credit card debt) to a lower debt option (e.g., personal loan).
3. Allocate any additional funds to one debt - either one with the larger interest or smallest balance. It is felt that paying the larger interest is the best financial decision; however,

paying the smallest debt allows you to get rid of one bill more quickly and creates momentum and confidence to tackle the others.

4. Stop adding more debt. You cannot borrow your way out of debt.

5. Increase your earnings. Every bit helps when you are deep in debt. Get a second job, a side hustle, pick up extra shifts, sell unused items and clothing. Do not let pride keep you in debt.

Of course, never go back to that place where debt resides. Learn to live frugally and within your means. Create an emergency fund, understand how you got where you are, and work on any underlying emotions that need to be managed.

DEBT SCHEDULE

MONEY IN	BUDGET	ACTUAL
EARNINGS		
ADDITIONAL INCOME		
TOTAL INCOME		

LOANS/MORTGAGES	TOTAL O/S	MONTHLY PMTS	YRS TO REPAY	DEBT RATIO	ACTUAL	MARKET
Mortgage						
Loan #1						
Loan #2						
Credit Card						
Store Card						
TOTAL EXPENSES						

MONEY LEFT OVER	BUDGET	ACTUAL
TOTAL EXPENSES		

DEBT-FREE LIVING

If you are on an accelerated money savings plan and financial independence trajectory, you may already be on a debt-free living path. Even if you are not, a debt-free life may be desirable to you.

There are different theories regarding whether living a debt-free life is being financially savvy, as there are benefits to having manageable levels of debt and using it as a method of increasing your net worth. Despite this, we know that financial decisions are made up of emotional behaviour and the choice of living a debt-free lifestyle is no different.

Living a debt-free lifestyle means your net worth is in the black, you owe nothing to financial institutions or individuals, and you have the ability to pay in cash when your balances become due.

If you are wondering about the benefits of living a debt-free lifestyle and what makes it so enticing, here are a few of the non-monetary ones:

1. **Reduced stress level:** Being able to rid yourself of the stress associated with debt and the strain it places on personal relationships is a huge factor.
2. **Living life on your terms:** Want to take a career break, cut back on work hours, take a demotion to lessen the stress load, retire early, or take the trip of a lifetime? A debt-free lifestyle makes these types of decisions easier.
3. **The ability to say "No":** Not having to worry about the ball-and-chain of debt, allows you to live a life that is congruent with who you are as a person and say "No" to things that do not bring you joy.
4. **Pivot:** At a young age, we make decisions about career paths to pursue, but somewhere along the way, life happens, and the result is that we do not always want to continue. With

stacks of debt behind you, it becomes much harder to pivot and choose a path that will bring you more joy. This can also relate to a desire to change locations. Having no debt holding you back will not only make it more possible, but it will also give you a chance to enjoy the experience much more.

5. **Life happens:** There is no doubt about this. Whether it is a car wreck, a health challenge, or a pandemic, with no debt, you are better able to handle emergencies and get back on track.

6. **Self-ownership:** The rich rule over the poor, and the borrower is servant to the lender (Proverbs 22:7). It is not always the debt that is the problem. In many cases, it is the conditions that come with that debt that present challenges. With every loan agreement you enter, whether to an organisation or an individual, you relinquish a portion of your life choices and freedom.

7. **Life choice:** No other reason than you do not like owing people.

8. **Gratitude:** Appreciation for the effort it takes to be able to live the life you desire, knowing you earned it by the sweat of your brow and sound decision making.

There are some characteristics that persons who live a debt-free lifestyle may possess:

1. They are non-materialistic. They share the view that no material item can trump the feeling of not going into debt. Some are even on a journey of minimalist-style living and do not have an attachment to *things*.

2. They like to chart their own path. Life is all about creating that unique adventure for yourself. Included in that should be your financial journey. Being debt-free means you will be able to live authentically and not worry about what other people are doing. You will not need to 'keep up with

the Jones" - because let us be real, the Jones' are in debt too.

3. Debt-free living harnesses discipline, a characteristic that stays with you. If you can master it, there will not be any area of your life where you will not see the benefits. Whether in your career, personal life, fitness, education or financial life, the ability to do what you say you are going to do each and every time, is a superpower.

4. Self-Confidence is another characteristic which is common among persons who are debt-free. Similar to living an authentic life and charting your own path, a debt-free lifestyle forces you to own your decisions, regardless of what the current acceptable norms are, and be confident. Driving a ten-year-old car that is paid for takes confidence, and most importantly, not feeling like you owe anyone an explanation for the lifestyle you have chosen. In the famous words of an old church lady from my childhood neighbourhood, "Please yourself and puzzle the world."

How to Live Debt-Free

1. **Budgeting and planning:** You do not escape the budget. It will become part of you and will eventually not be called a 'budget' but your way of life. Knowing your credit card cutoff date and choosing to make a purchase *after* that cutoff date, rather than right now to get the maximum time to repay without incurring any finance charges, is one of the many ways you can leverage your financial knowledge when you are organised.

2. **Emergency funds:** This is what hardcore financial adulting looks like - having funds set aside for large purchases or emergencies before they happen, therefore reducing the need to borrow money. It can be as simple as having the funds to pay for your car or house insurance when it is due by setting it aside beforehand; or it can be knowing a car or

major appliance is of a certain age, will need replacing, and setting aside the funds to do that before it happens.

3. **Sinking funds:** For the average adult, these can include yearly home and car insurance, home and car maintenance, household appliances, travel, birthdays, holidays, and/or new or replacement electronics. As an experienced budgeter, these categories will eventually become part of your annual budget instead of an external exercise done separately.

4. **Authenticity:** Once again, this word has popped up. Stay in your own money lane. There is no need to prove any point to anyone. There is no need to do what anyone else is doing. Being honest about what activities and expenses you can take on, will keep you on the debt-free path.

5. **Long-term goals:** Integrating long-term goals into your lifestyle will help you keep focused on your path. Knowing where your ultimate journey is leading you and why you are determined to embark on this type of lifestyle, is critical.

6. **Increasing your revenue or creating additional streams of revenue:** This is not necessary on a debt-free path, but it may be necessary for you to get on that path in the first place. If you are carrying debt with final repayment far down the road, it will take more effort.

7. **Don't buy '*ish*' you don't need:** This *should* fall in line with living an authentic life, but that is not always the case. You can be on your own path and still fall prey to consumerism, buying things you do not really need. Consumerism is at an all-time high. Everywhere you turn, there is an ad or influencer trying to get you to part ways with your hard-earned money. Being conscious of what you are consuming, whether via social media, television or even in-person, will prevent you from buying things you do not really need.

8. **Increase your financial knowledge:** Get financially savvy by understanding how interest is calculated on loans and credit cards. Learn how to use credit cards, the benefits

without the debt, the best time to make certain large purchases, and understand marketing strategies to avoid paying more for an item on sale (when it is really $5 more than it was *before* the sale—if you did not know, companies actually do that).

9. **Practice delayed gratification:** This is one of my all-time favourite practices. You know that game you play where you leave an item and see how you feel about it in a few days? You can use this as a method of reward for yourself for hitting a milestone on a journey. A few years ago, while going through an extended pay increase "situation," I saw a relatively inexpensive piece of jewellery I wanted. I decided I would not purchase it until I had won the battle. The battle I am referring to occurred when I was thrust into a position at work which had not been discussed with me prior. To make matters more interesting, I was not being compensated for the extra duties. It took a few months, but once the battle was won, I made the purchase. Now, when I wear that piece of jewellery, it is a reminder to always stay the course and not allow others to take advantage of me nor my efforts.

10. **Embrace the joy of living without spending:** Learn to enjoy your life without needing to spend money all day, every day. Find activities that do not need money to be spent. This may also lead to a slow down and appreciation for the simple things or it may bring a reconnection to activities you once participated in but had forgotten.

CHAPTER 8
INCREASE YOUR EARNINGS

For many, employment is the main source of income. The level of income that is paid to us is not of our own choosing, but what is offered to us by the decision-makers of the company we work for, which we have the choice to reject or accept.

Many will suggest that you cannot attain financial security and wealth by working for someone else. That theory is dependent upon where you sit, because there are many people who *do* earn multi-million-dollar packages per year from being an employee, and there are others who have used the money earned from their nine-to-five to create substantial empires.

Regardless of whether you have a multimillion-dollar package or a much smaller one, as an employee, there are ways you can increase your earnings.

CONTINUOUS DEVELOPMENT

"In times of change, learners inherit the earth, while the learned find

themselves beautifully equipped to deal with a world that no longer exists."
~Eric Hoffer~

The best pay increase you will ever give yourself comes from continuous development, both academic and non-academic. Many moons ago, companies invested heavily in the education and training of their employees. Back then, employees were lifers and companies also gained from the training and education it funded.

But those training budgets went away two recessions ago and will not be back anytime soon (at least not in any meaningful way). Additionally, thanks to the current and upcoming population of working persons who are unwilling to provide blind loyalty to companies, there is no incentive for companies to increase their training budgets at this point. Your development is your responsibility. The idea that a company or another person should heavily invest in your future for your gain, is an exceptionally entitled attitude.

A few years ago, I sat in a staff meeting aghast as one employee explained their frustration that the company was unwilling to pay for training - training unrelated to the company's line of business. What this employee wanted was for their personal development.

The most shocking thing about the conversation was that 80% of the people in the room agreed with them. There was so much to learn from that discussion, and it drove home the reason why people are in the same jobs for over twenty years, and still cannot manage the basic tasks associated with their daily jobs. It was clear this person did not see their own development as *their* job, but that of the company they worked for.

Let me be clear. I am not absolving companies of their responsibility to train staff, because quite frankly, many companies are currently doing a substandard job in this area and even failing in the basic onboarding process. With that said, why are you still sitting waiting for a company to invest in *you*? Why are you putting the responsibility to propel your career and increase your earnings in someone else's hands? Your focus should be on vertical movement, and the way to make those moves and keep yourself in the game, is by continuously developing yourself.

Pay increases related to inflation will not help you change your life trajectory. All they do is help you maintain the same standard of living you currently have, and that is only if the increase you receive actually matches the current inflation rate.

Let's be honest. If you are currently sitting in the Caribbean, pay increases for inflation rates are afforded to very few in some sectors and are a completely foreign concept to most of the working population. There are many in the working population who have not had a pay adjustment for over ten years. Because of this, it is imperative that you keep striving to increase your worth through development.

However, it would be reckless of me to try to sell you a dream, making you believe that because you have invested in an expensive course or advanced degree, that it will automatically translate to an increase in pay. Unfortunately, that is not the case.

Additional education, like every other aspect of your life, must come with a strategic plan. You must ensure you are not throwing money away and that there will be an acceptable level of return. An advanced degree without any experience is just an expensive piece of paper. You must still be willing to dig in and get the work experience, to put the theoretical aspects of your training into practise.

Also, do not overlook those soft skills which are not acquired in a classroom, and do not believe that the only way to increase your value is through financial investment. There are many free courses, readings, and videos that can help you be a more rounded person. The Internet is a gold mine if you are willing to take time and find useful resources.

The best part about self-betterment is that it is 's *yours*. You will never lose it, and no one can ask for it to be returned. Furthermore, whether you continue in your current career, switch careers, or opt for early retirement, the gift of self-investment will always be a part of you. There is also the feeling of achievement you will have knowing you put in the hard work and can enjoy the fruits of your labour. Mostly, you did what many are unwilling to do: you bet on yourself, and you won the prize.

Clap for your-damn-self!

BET ON YOURSELF

Risk equals rewards. *Calculated* risk, that is.

The only way you will bet small and win big, is if you win the lottery, and the chances of that happening are 1 in 14 million.

Let me tell you a story about calculated risk. Many years ago, newly out of university, I was on my way to a job interview, travelling by public transport. I had given myself enough time to arrive punctually (or so I thought), but after waiting for more than an hour for the bus, I was scarily late. The bus eventually arrived and as I sat watching each minute pass, I knew there was no way I was going to make it on time.

With each stop to pick up and set off more passengers, I got more worked up. I decided I was going to take a calculated risk and get off the bus. I knew that by sitting there, it would be impossible to make the time, but if I got off and some miracle happened, I might make it, or it could all go horribly wrong, and I would end up being even later. I got off the bus, and a stranger gave me a ride to the front door of the company.

Let me add some context to this story.

I was not unemployed at the time, but was looking for a more progressive role. I could have simply given up or been nonchalant about the time, but that is not in my nature.

Plot twist - I did not end up taking the job, but the fact is, from that calculated risk, I gave myself a chance. If you are unwilling to go all-in for yourself, you are going to come up short. Whether it is time, energy, or money, you must do it for you. When there is no one there to help and the road ahead seems daunting, or when no one believes in your ideas, you must somehow dig deep and keep going.

Once you start your ascension, you will realise that the road ahead becomes less congested and that is because most people are only willing to go so far and do so much before fear or some other self-disparaging theory kicks in. If you are willing to stay the course and have a plan of action, you will see the rewards. If you consistently show up and are willing to align yourself with your truth, the law of attraction will deliver for you. We all start somewhere, whether with external assistance or pure talent, and at some point, we are going to falter. We must be prepared for when that happens and must know how to come back to the core of who we are to get back on track.

"You must have long-term goals to keep you from getting frustrated short-term"
~Charles C Noble~

BE OF VALUE

Successful businesses understand the concept of adding value. When customers pay for a product or service, there is a certain expectation that comes with that purchase, but going *beyond* the customer's expectations is what keeps them coming back. That same theory can be applied to your working career. Adding value to any room or organisation you enter, keeps you employed and on the "ninety-nine problems, but a job ain't one" train.

You know that one person in the organisation who is consulted, regardless of whether the issue falls into their core competencies?

Not to be confused with the person who withholds information or implements useless controls so all roads lead to them, but the level-headed, calm individual who knows something about almost everything, who is capable of getting the job done without fanfare, who has the ability to see the forest for the trees and can do all that in a very uncomplicated and unbiased way. That is who I am talking about.

Those people have the ability to stay the course and reap the long-term rewards whilst rarely appearing in the spotlight. They are well-aware that likability is overrated and short-lived.

If you want to forge an illustrious career, then focus on being of value. It is the best public relations campaign you can give yourself because if done correctly, you will never have to look for another job in your life. The opportunities will present themselves to you. My theory is, they do not have to like you, but they should respect your craft. Your craft is what keeps you fed.

Be unashamedly good at your job and do that by focusing on perfecting your craft. Never be afraid to learn what you do not know and never consider any pieces of work to be below your level. Understand the foundational elements of your job. Should a crisis occur, or should you need to step down from your current level, unemployment will not be your reality. Rather, you will be able to take on a role at a lower level, even if temporarily.

NOT LEAVING MONEY ON THE TABLE

1. Utilising Programmes and Benefits

Many times, we look at the dollar-value of a job and base its worth on that, without a deep consideration of the perks that could accompany it, such as stock benefits, extra vacation or rest days, payment for overseas training programs, refunds for educational courses, travel expenses - the list goes on.

Companies save and waste a ton of money annually, simply because employees do not take advantage of the benefits offered to them. One that always sticks out to me, as the owner of the budget for many companies over the years, are the services of employee assistance programs (EAPs). Most mid-sized to large companies pay external companies to provide these services. Sadly, many of them are grossly underused. As a matter of fact, in previous roles I have held, decisions to reduce the package level of services were made, simply because the usage was so dismal, the company was wasting money.

There seems to be a rejection of EAPs from the general staff, which may be linked to distrust. There might also be a lack of understanding regarding how they work and the fact that the service is of a confidential nature. In some cases, companies are obligated to provide these services, as stated by the law. Whatever the situation, EAPs and the services they offer, are there for the taking as part of your employment, and in the world we currently live in, are needed now more than ever.

If your work environment is contributing to your stress, why not use the resources paid for by that company to help the situation?

2. Training Programmes

In a well-run company, the employee manual will list the benefits offered, but in many companies it is a grey area. No one really knows where the company stands as it relates to certain benefits, or it is at the discretion of one individual, and many times, you do not know until you ask.

Yes, there is a lot to be learned from simply asking a question. The most one can say is "no," in which case, you know; but the answer may be "yes." It should be noted that a "yes" may come with some conditions.

3. Shares/Retirement/Savings Plans

There are many who will sing praises about these types of programmes, and if you have ever wondered why there are some people who stay in a not-so-great working environment for many years, one of them may be the reason.

In the "good ole' days" (as some former coworkers of mine would say), these programmes provided down payment for houses, assisted in employees being able to build their homes without debt and provided funding for their offspring's university education. In today's environment, however, these programmes are barely in existence, and many do not filter down to the average worker. Some are like wolves in sheep's clothing because while it appears to benefit the staff, the rewards are so paltry it is laughable.

The onus is on each employee to ensure they understand these programs if they are being offered, determine how they can benefit from them, and engage in the same decision-making process they use when considering their goals. If you do not have the financial understanding to determine the best choice, seek assistance outside your company, especially when changes are being made to the current plans.

Your priority should always be to make sure the financial decisions being made are beneficial to you and your long-term objectives. Do not simply assume the company will take care of your individual interest.

PAY INCREASES

Let us address this elephant in the room, but first, let me state that I am sure my thoughts here are going to be biased, ruthless, and based on my life experiences; and as the commercials state: **All testimonials are from real participants and individual results may vary. Testimonials may not represent typical results, reflect the typical purchaser's experience, and are not intended to represent or guarantee that anyone will achieve the same or similar results.**

Now that we have that out of the way...

Over the years, I have heard people say, if you take a job at a particular rate, then you cannot expect to be paid more for that job later. I wholeheartedly disagree.

I also think that people who make those kinds of statements have not worked outside of their environment. They have never been exposed to the concept of plying their trade outside their countries as an expat, or in a market where there is an abundance of talent and limited job options.

They also do not have much experience in the world of corporate BS, because I do not care what number you have when you walk through that door—you can walk out with a higher one. In the last twenty years, I have secured pay increases from 5% to 65%, all within less than two years of entering the building. Actually, within one year. The 65% was the accumulation of three increases in less than two years, which was the end result of some peculiar circumstances.

Now firstly, as a junior person trying to get into any field when there is not much differentiation between candidates (aka, university graduates with little or no experience), the employers have the market, and they know that. Over the years, as more and more graduates have entered the market, the salary and benefits have dwindled. This is nothing new and has been happening since the beginning of time. If you are really focused on building a career and earning experience, you will take a job. Be wise. Secure one that offers the opportunity to earn experience and do not focus on the pay cheque. Of course, make certain you can pay your bills.

The old folks in Barbados would say, "First trick ain't no trick." Yes, you will be aware that the company is in the driver's seat, and you need to be okay with that. What matters most is that you have gotten your foot in the door. Prove yourself and put the ball back in their court. Either they will see your worth or they will not. If they do, a pay increase will come and if they do not, you will take the experience earned elsewhere for a better rate. This is business, not friendship.

The individuals who understand this well are expats. Let me speak from my truth and point of view - black and minority expats. More specifically, female, black expats, because each one of those words have a different discounted pay rate. It is not a matter of *if* you are going to be short-changed at some point. It is a matter of *by how much*.

Expats are there to fill a void in a market which cannot be filled with the current labour force in that market. Unless it is for a very highly specialised area, when companies attempt to fill that void internationally, there are plenty of options available. The world is one big marketplace, and many do not understand this, because they do not see past their own environment.

The competition to secure that first contract can be fierce, but once you have, you can leverage your opportunities. I know in some cases the opportunity to earn an expat salary is life-changing for both the individual and their families, and many will not want to speak up for fear of losing it. While I have referenced this topic from an expat's point of view, this is also relevant in any local market where there are more people than jobs. Do not be afraid to go back to the table.

Early on in my career, I decided I would not belittle myself to ask any company for a pay increase, even though I knew I was deserving. If they did not see my worth, that was on them. In one of my earlier experiences, I took on a lower-level role to get into the market. Within three months of starting, the company indicated they recognised I was hired at too low a level and a promotion was in the cards. The pay increase with that promotion was a slap in the face. It simultaneously came at a time when I was designated as a systems expert with additional responsibility, but the elevated position meant that, according to company policy, I would not receive additional pay for that added title.

Sometime after, it was suggested I should spend my day training my charges, as it was deemed there was a lack of skills within the team I had inherited. It was also suggested that when said charges went home in the evenings, I should then do my own work. Adding context to this, the training was really teaching basic accounting and business procedures, such as debits, credits, and basic Excel skills. Considering this was far from being a company with a culture of overwork (this company had a culture where Friday pub lunches were at least two hours), I found this suggestion to be insulting. So, I took up my Georgie bundle and headed out. A substantial pay increase and decrease in responsibility from the next gig I secured, showed how inconsiderate that situation was.

In the latter part of my career, I did a 360 about asking for what I deserve and here is why. Years ago, one of my male counterparts told me that the difference between him and me was, "I'll make them pay through their arse." That is not the full reason, but that stayed with me over the years.

My position is, when a company sells me a dream that turns into a nightmare, the original contract becomes null and void and we are going to have to go back to the table. While this is not the expected situation, it is quite prevalent and more so in some sectors than others. Hospitality is one of them. I could completely go off-track at this point and write an entire book on that sector alone, but let us stay focused.

If you sign an agreement to move A, B, and C, and then all the other letters of the alphabet suddenly appear, head back to the table. There will be times we take on additional work to earn experience, assist co-workers, help with a transition or whatever is needed at the time to help the boat stay afloat, but there is a difference between that and giving away your labour for free.

In the current work culture of overwork, there are many people doing jobs which were designed for two or more people, and I know because I have been there myself. I also know it will lead you nowhere other than towards ill-health and burn out; and you had better believe you will need those dollars to pay those doctors', therapist, and masseuse bills. Always remember, health is wealth. You cannot be afraid to ask for compensation which matches the work and responsibility you are carrying. If a company is unwilling to pay you a fair rate for your labour, then that tells you how they feel about you. Besides, it is better to know how they *really* feel than to wonder, and once an increase in remuneration gets put on the table, trust me, you will know how they *really* feel. While your feelings may be hurt by an unfavourable decision, it is better to know. Remember, this is business, not friendship.

Let us also talk about recognition. There is a stark distinction between recognition and compensation and the two do not always happen concurrently. Being recognised for the additional effort you put in daily should not replace the need to be compensated for such efforts. Plaques and awards are great, but you cannot use them to pay for groceries at the supermarket. The doctor does not accept accolades as compensation for his work, and cars use gas and diesel, which require money.

Fresh-faced out of university, I was given a letter of commendation for taking on a task at the last minute and excelling within a very stringent timeline. This was not the first time I had done it, but the timeline on this occasion was deemed unlikely, and I managed to pull it off. During the discussion with my superiors at the time, I cheekily said, "So, does that mean I'll get a pay increase too?" Despite having just randomly blurted that out, I walked away with an additional $100/month. It was said to be the cap on the position, and I gracefully accepted it. I took that role to gain experience, so a rejection would not have mattered, but according to my Bajan fore-parents, "Closed mouths don't get fed." So, I asked.

Before we get carried away thinking we are out there simply asking for extra money because we are bold enough to and can secure it, understand that it requires putting in work for many years to be in a position where you can ultimately be bold enough to walk the path of saying, "This is what I bring to the table, this is what I am currently doing and this is what I am worth."

To get to this point, it takes years of honing your craft, staying focused on your career and lots of self-development. During these years, your priority should be on the experience you are gathering and not just the actual pay you are earning. The increase in value will accompany an increase in pay, but should you focus only on pay, you will hit a wall at an early stage.

While you may be able to increase your compensation by a few hundred dollars a month through measures that may be effortless and non-strategic in the short-term, that amount can easily be eaten up by inflation or lifestyle changes. What you really want to focus on is strategic moves that will elevate you vertically.

At this point, let me add some more truth, get real and not sell you a dream, because you may put in the work, go the extra mile and prove your worth, and it still does not mean you are going to be rewarded within your current company. If only the world worked like that, we would all live a blissfully simple life. Decisions are made by people and people are going to be people. As an adult, hopefully you understand that we do not always get what we want from who we want it from.

This is where emotional intelligence comes into play. Before you approach a company for an increase in compensation or during the interview phase, you must know at what point you are willing to walk away. Of course, this does not apply to those starting out in the field and/or unemployed with limited options. The focus here is on seasoned people who have earned the right to command a particular pay. This is why I am a strong advocate of having money in the bank, because without knowing how your bills are going to be paid, it becomes extremely difficult to keep your integrity and lessens your chances of being able to walk away when the situation does not appeal to you.

The thing with this game is, yes, much of it is a game. Your employers have also done an assessment and determined what they are willing to offer, and have an idea of what they think it will take to satisfy you. They also use their judgment to decide whether they think you have the guts to actually walk away. They do not always get this right, and the reason is some decision makers assume that people need a job and that, in these uncertain times, they would rather have something than nothing. When they encounter people who do not fit that mould, they are left up a creek without a paddle. If you are someone who lives a financial life which allows you to walk away from the table, you can boldly and bravely call your number.

NEGOTIATION

It is often said that women are not good negotiators. My theory is that women should not have to negotiate for things that are readily given to their male counterparts for the same role and experience. Quite frankly, I am not a fan of negotiating simply because I believe it to be a waste of time. I also think it can feel quite degrading. Companies come to the table already knowing the maximum they are willing to offer, and employees should know the least they are willing to take. I deem that dance to the middle ground to be a waste of my precious time.

When a company chooses to nickel and dime, it tells you who they are and it is very hard to change that perception going forward. As a black expat, I have seen that nickel and dime to be as little as $5k - $15k per year, which translates to $5 per hour, which is about the equivalent of the bill for the company sponsored drinks event.

While a senior executive may feel proud of themselves for an amount that will not impact some companies' bottom line, for an expat that can be the difference in the move being worth their while or a change in circumstance for their family at home.

Let us do some quick math.

$10k USD translates to approximately $20k Barbados Dollars, $27k Eastern Caribbean Dollars, $1.5m Jamaican Dollars or $4m Nigerian Naira - yet the expectation is that persons will go beyond the call of duty, working excessive hours by doing their share of work and picking up the slack of others after being nickelled and dimed during the hiring process.

During the mid-part of my career, I made some requests on a short-term contract. I indicated to the company that I was unwilling to get on the plane without some basics, such as medical insurance. The recruiter for the role indicated that they had never seen so many benefits added to a short-term contract.

I found it quite disturbing; firstly, that these benefits needed to be asked for, and secondly, that the recruiter was not trying to secure the best deal for me. This was a lesson I learnt late (or rather did not learn it as well as I should have the first time) and therefore it came back to me. The length of the contract was of no importance. Nothing I had requested was out of the ordinary, as I have seen several contracts with these benefits before and one can only ponder why they were not included in the first place.

Over the years, I have learned to call my number and sit in silence, because good labour is not cheap and cheap labour is not good. When you cheat yourself, people do not respect what you bring to the table. You have to let them know to put some respect on the work you do by attaching some zeros to those numbers. In some cases, as they counter your offer, they will want to add everything (including the kitchen sink) to your duties simply because they had to offer a fair rate. Hold your ground and sit in that silence. It will get uncomfortable, but always remember, one should never negotiate with the devil. When a company shows you who they are, you had better believe them.

My distaste for negotiating was fuelled when I travelled in Asia for four months, and also adds to my dislike of southern Thailand. I have no desire to get out of bed every day and be in the streets haggling from breakfast to dinner. Who has time for that? It is exhausting and annoying.

My first night in Thailand, I saw a street vendor selling some nicely cut up mangoes. I indicated I wanted to purchase some. He took one look at me and plucked a number from the sky. I honestly thought I had not heard him properly, so I asked him to repeat the cost. Then I recalculated the currency rate in my head and said, "For mango?" He started to grumble. The giveaway was his teenage son, who looked like he wanted the earth to swallow him up out of embarrassment. I walked off and left the man with the mango in his hand, while he shouted obscenities at me. I will never understand why people shout profanity in languages I do not speak when I am in foreign countries - as if they think I am above responding to them with Bajan curse words.

Anyhow, negotiating *still* is not my cup of tea, but in this world, we are going to have to ask for what we deserve.

ADVOCATE FOR YOURSELF

You must be willing to be your biggest cheerleader. Expecting someone else to lead the charge on your behalf to benefit you is naïve. Why should another individual advocate on your behalf if you are not willing to do it for yourself? That kind of advocacy should be left for minors and the vulnerable in our community. As for the rest of us, we need to step up for ourselves.

Let me share a secret. Regardless of what the employee manual or the company policy states, there are always anomalies. Why? Because those people are advocating for themselves, and the company bought into it. Are they the hardest workers? Not always. Are they the most experienced? Probably not. They are simply bold enough to ask for what they want, and they receive it.

Decisions made are not always going to be in your favour, mainly because the company officer's objective is to protect the company's assets. Businesses are created to earn financial gains. If it does not make money, it does not make sense. Regardless of how good a corporate citizen a company is, the primary objective is to make money.

Another factor you need to consider (and the most important one) is that companies are made up of *people*. Whether it is an individual owner or a body of executives, the decisions are being made by human beings and, as I always say, human beings are going to be human beings. Emotions will factor into any decision, and whether we want to admit it or not, human beings are biased.

There will always be a reason to give employee 'A' additional benefits that employee 'B' will not be receiving. Again, they are not always monetary or reasons to refuse a pay increase, stipend, or a fair rate. They are simply based on nothing more than the reality that the decision maker does not want to for that particular employee.

As we now live in a world where discrimination is illegal in many places, there will be some wishy-washy explanations and other tactics employed, which can range from trying to trivialise your contribution and experience to openly stating that you are lucky to have earned a seat at the table. These objections are raised to justify their actions, which is even more reason why you have to advocate for yourself.

Many employees are fearful of having open communication about things that affect them and would rather whisper among themselves than speak up. It is not always about pay. It could also be about work conditions and company culture, as these also contribute to a healthy work environment. Whispering to your coworkers or bending your friends' and family members' ears is not going to help. If you want something done, then you are going to have to be bold enough to step up and speak up.

Expecting other individuals to speak on your behalf is like handing your future to someone else. Sure, some people may do it, but are they going to truly represent your best interests? Whilst it may appear that an individual has some influence and can use it to help you, they themselves may be fighting their own battles. Your immediate manager may be trying to reach to the next level, which may mean they will not always be advocating for you behind closed doors. They may be trying to push their own agenda, and rightfully so. The onus is on you to use your voice and speak up on your behalf.

Let us also open the can of worms. Many black women and minorities who have made it into the room or to the table are fighting for their lives on a daily basis, trying to keep their already earned place. It is laborious and unrealistic for them to carry everyone else. Furthermore, it should not be expected.

We must be bold enough to take the steps necessary to elevate ourselves. If we are afraid of taking these steps, we are afraid of growing and winning. Life is not going to hand you anything for free.

Some people may be fortunate recipients of such gifts, but the fact is, for most of us, we are going to have to work for it.

KEEP YOUR STANDARDS HIGH AND YOUR 'VEX MONEY' HIGHER

Back in the day, it was common to hear older women talking about having *vex money*, and it was tradition for this information to be passed on to the younger women when they deemed them old enough to understand the concept. *Vex money* was the money a woman had in her purse whilst going on a date or other occasions, in case there was a falling out or she felt unsafe and had to make her own way home.

That same energy should be carried through life. There will come a time in life when a situation does not serve you, whether it is a job, a business deal, or a personal relationship. If you are going to continue being true to yourself and maintain your integrity and standards, you are going to have to make the decision to walk away.

When you are at that boardroom table and the decisions being made are not in your best interest; when the decisions being made puts your integrity into question; when you are being taken advantage of; when your contribution is being trivialised and downtrodden; when the promotion you have been promised suddenly disappears, you are going to want to give yourself that option. The only way you will be able to do that is by making sure you have your bag secured and your bills paid.

It is exceedingly difficult to maintain your standards and integrity when you do not know how your bills are going to be paid or how you will put food on the table. People will try to take advantage of you and treat you like less than a person when they know your options are limited. Do not hand that power over to anyone.

Over the course of my career, I have walked away from many situations. No job is ever worth my peace, integrity, or mental health.

In the accounting profession, once your integrity has been questioned, it is extremely hard to recoup it. Whether an illegal act was committed or not, it is the stain that comes after. While some business decisions are not always illegal, many of them are immoral and at the end of the day, one should always be able to look at themselves in the mirror, have their family and friends look at them with respect, and be able to sleep well at night.

How many times have you heard someone say, "I would never do that," or, "If that were to happen to me, I'd never tolerate it!" - and the list goes on. Until all those things *do* happen and the person they never thought they would be is the person they are. Why? Because the bills do not pay themselves.

As Mike Tyson said, "Everybody has a plan until they get punched in the mouth."

CHAPTER 9
SELF-EMPLOYMENT

Some make the bold decision to create their income through self-employment. This decision could be a result of a dream come true or necessity. Recessions create a slew of new businesses because of the downsizing of jobs available in the traditional job market.

It was reported that 800,000 additional businesses were started in the US during 2020. The reasons for the increase ranged from persons losing their jobs, persons having time at home to focus on projects and goals they had placed on the back burner, persons discovering talent they had as a result of having time to find themselves, and persons finally feeling brave enough to step out after being reminded of how fragile life can be.

In this chapter, I will share my experience as a small business owner, the lessons learned and the harsh truths we all need to acknowledge if we are going to successfully earn a living by means of self-employment.

When people think of starting a small business, there are two questions they have on their minds: how do I know what kind of business I should start and where do I begin? Regarding the first question, the answer is, look within. Most businesses are birthed out of a person's love for a particular area. This might be a hobby. It is a good idea if you are eager to supplement your income with some extra cash and not necessarily to create a business to replace your main income. Recognising a void in the market is also another sound reason for business development.

The advantage of developing a hobby into a commercial activity is that you are sure to have fun because it is an area you enjoy. In 2013, I created an agribusiness which mirrored my love of gardening. While I will not purport it to be a massive success, I got to spend time doing something I love. It supported my gardening habit and gave me the ability to create an additional stream of income. I was able to eat the produce I grew and, most importantly, I got my feet wet in the start-up field at a manageable pace.

How I stumbled upon this gap in the market was because of trying to grow the best tomatoes possible on my patio. While researching an issue I was having, I found a fabric container with advanced technology and decided to try it. During the process of deciding how many to order for my personal use, I concluded that if I was having this issue, surely there were other people who did as well. There was a void in the market.

My order went from a few single pots for myself to a few boxes of assorted sizes and I soon had a new start-up business. I was also a sole practitioner with my own accounting services business at the time. Let me be honest and say, it did not occur to me that I had been running two start-up small businesses, as I did not consider being a self-employed accountant a start-up; however, as time went by, I discovered what I had gotten myself into.

SIDE BUSINESS, HUSTLE OR START-UP COMPANY

At the earliest opportunity, once you have found the business idea you wish to pursue, you should decide what business model it fits into. In other words, is your 'business' a side business, a hustle, or a true start-up company? This is important to consider, since every decision you make will be determined by this. Of course, there is also the hybrid option, as many facets of life these days fall into this multidimensional category.

Let us discuss the pros and cons of each business model.

1. **Side business** - a business created as another stream of income. Its purpose is not necessarily to replace the main source of income, but to be profitable enough to stand on its own and contribute to the overall objective of building wealth.

Pros of a Side Business

1. Used as an additional source of income.
2. A legally registered entry with limited liability.
3. Create generational wealth.
4. Opportunity to create passive income.
5. Opportunity to divest investment.

Cons of a Side Business

1. Dedicating time to growing the business.
2. Funding and resources needed to start.
3. Motivation to create business longevity.
4. Managing business partnerships and fallouts.
5. Effort to seek knowledge needed to manage the business.

2. **Hustle** - a quick buck scheme, generating cash quickly without many resources to fill a short-term financial need.

Pros of a Hustle

1. Don't need many resources to get started.
2. Quick results to fill a financial gap.
3. No additional education required.

Cons of a Hustle

1. Feeds you for a day, not a lifetime.
2. Market becomes saturated quickly.
3. Usually, non-passive type income.
4. Heavily dependent on supply and demand.
5. Profits unstable and unsure.

3. **Start-up Company** - created to supply long-term financial gains, replacing the main source of income.

Pros of a Start-up Company

1. Create long-term income.
2. Opportunity to achieve life goals.
3. Opportunity to buy back freedom.
4. Potential to move to large-scale business.

Cons of a Start-up Business

1. Statistics of businesses who make it long-term.
2. Knowledge needed to succeed.
3. Staying the course.
4. Use of external resources to scale up.

Once you have established the type of business venture you are going to pursue, it is then time to create a plan. Based on your decision, you may need to register a business name or incorporate the company, hire an attorney to create business agreements, open a bank account for the business and other start-up tasks.

You should ensure you are familiar with the statutory requirements needed and obligations you are required to fulfill. Failure to educate yourself on these types of affairs can be detrimental to the success of your business.

Too many small business owners start businesses without the basic knowledge of business structure, statutory requirements, basic financial knowledge, and even understanding banking procedures. Business mistakes can be costly, and you run the risk of losing a business you have worked hard to create, because you signed agreements you did not fully understand. Perhaps you got into it without legal agreements or failed to fulfill statutory obligations and much more.

You also run the risk of losing financial investments such as a home you may have had before the business venture because of failing to ring-fence your business liability or not understanding the risk of using your investment as collateral (either for your own business or that of another individual). During this process, your personal credit ratings or reputation can be ruined if you fail to supply products and services or are unable to service your financial obligations.

Strategy and Planning

Before you attempt to trade your product and service, a strategic business plan should be produced. This does not have to be a twelve-page document complete with graphics and perfection, but you must create a basic business plan so you know where you are going and how you are going to get there.

Where many small business owners fail, is by assuming that business plans are only needed if they are seeking external funding. By doing so, they fail to determine whether the business venture is even financially viable. Whether or not you need financial resources from external sources, you should create at least three years' worth of financial projections before you decide whether to proceed.

You also need to create a marketing and business development strategy. There is nothing worse than bringing a great product or service to market and then not being able to secure sales because no thought was put into how you will get the news out about your existence. Or because you have no idea about the market conditions you are operating in, and which advertising channels will work best for your type of product or service.

I do not believe anyone gets into business fully having all the knowledge they need, and there is a learning curve that will take place even for seasoned businesspersons as the markets ebb and flow. However, by failing to map out a plan, you give yourself less of a chance to create a successful business.

START-UP ON A BUDGET

"I want to start a business, but funding is so hard to come by," - words I hear time and time again. My question becomes, what do you need funding to do? Usually, the responses have nothing to do with the actual production of a service or product for the start-up business but more of maintaining oneself whilst the business is in its infancy stage.

The romanticising of entrepreneurship gives people the impression they need more start-up capital for a small business than they actually do. There is the grandeur of business ownership which involves an office or warehouse space, fancy e-commerce websites, plush vehicles, and freedom with one's time, which causes individuals to attempt to walk before they have learned how to crawl.

The focus should not be on trying to look fancy and established, but on providing your service or products in a professional manner that allows the business to grow into a well-established company in the long-term. A fancy e-commerce website or a plush office does not translate to actual revenue. If you are unable to secure sales, all you will be left with is mounting bills, and this is where the capital you think you need will end up going.

In 2011, when I started my business accounting service company, my intent was to start up on a shoestring budget with a professional appearance. I believe I accomplished that with a little external help and some elbow grease.

Here are a few tips:

1. Engage a professional to create a logo that becomes the symbol of your business. People may not always remember your name, but they *will* attach you to a logo.

On a shoestring budget, skip the big firms and use a budding designer. Acknowledge that they will not have all the experience in the world, and approach them having an idea of what you want (e.g., colours and concept). Let them provide you with a few options to choose from. Understand that perfectionism is for the birds and do not be a pain in the ass, especially if you have no idea what you want. If you do not know, how can they? If you are unable to help them to help you, you need to engage the services of a firm or individual with years of experience and pay for it. Translate that logo to every aspect of your business - cards, websites, invoices, receipts, and apparel for visibility.

2. Research any benefits that you or your business would be entitled to and pursue them. This might include refunds or rebates, duty-free concessions, and tax reductions. Do not expect them to be offered to you, and do not expect the process to be easy. Accessing these benefits can be extremely frustrating as many are offered through governmental and quasi-governmental organisations and the inconsistency and incompetence which is encountered is astonishing.

I remember sitting outside a government department while seeking a concession that the regulations stated I could apply for. I overheard the employees pleading with the departmental head to grant me the status. I did not know these ladies, but the fact they felt I should have the same opportunities afforded to the big businesses was extremely humbling. That was my third visit to the department, and I was granted permission that day.

Unfortunately, we are forced to operate business in an environment that is inconsistent, antiquated, and oppressive. As a result, things are not always as simple as they should be. As a new business owner, when your surname does not suggest that the fee of success has already been paid on your behalf, you are going to have to be persistent and advocate for yourself. Every now and then, the universe will send a few angels to help you along the journey, because, Lord knows, all this advocating is exhausting.

3. Utilise or build personal skills that will help you save money. These may be website creation, flyer creation, digital marketing, or bookkeeping. If you do not currently possess any of these skills, you can learn the basics via free resources like YouTube, your local community centre or college.

In 2009, I enrolled in a web design course, as it was a skill that interested me, and I figured it would come in handy. At the time, a visiting colleague suggested that it made no sense why a Chartered accountant would do such. They were of the opinion that the two hours on Saturday mornings were best spent in the office, even though I was already spending many Saturday afternoons there.

I carried on in my usual stance of 'please yourself and puzzle the world'. Fast forward to the time when I required a business website. At that point, I did not want to dedicate the man-hours it would require to build my own website (even though I knew how), neither did I have the confidence. However, when I was provided with a quote for someone else to build a static website for me, I had designed a draft website myself within forty-eight hours.

It appeared as though I simply needed some motivation.

4. Determine which organisations or network groups best suit your business type and your intentions as a businessperson. There are a few to choose from and most will come with some level of admission fee and/or yearly subscription. Many may not be worth the price or the time. Manage your expectations of what networking will look like within these organisations. In some cases, you will find membership and business relationships are contingent upon the level of acquaintance, and *strangers* are left in the cold until they prove their worthiness.

5. Spend the time to create and document your process. It will be worth it as the company starts to grow. Additionally, should you expand and need to hire employees, the blueprint will be there. Create templates for standard email responses, quotes, estimates, and requests for proposals. You do not want to miss opportunities or deadlines because you are spinning in mud and reinventing the wheel each time. Likewise, create a list of your services/products which are not of a bespoke nature and price them. This will facilitate your response time and the appearance of having a well-run machine.

6. Get your hands dirty. Research your market. Get out there and speak to people. Do not expect to find everything you need on the Internet and do not expect customers to come looking for you. Be willing to take your product or service from idea directly to the customer. This ensures people can associate you with the product or service, even if your name eludes them. Building the kind of brand awareness that translates to new customers and clients takes time - a lot longer than you may think.

THE HARSH TRUTH ABOUT BUSINESS ON A SMALL ISLAND

Talent and hard work are *supposedly* the recipe for success; that is, unless you are trying to do business within small island states. In such a scenario, the business environment can be described more as a society where you unintentionally apply to join a secret club, and approval is based on whether the members determine you to be worthy enough of earning a decent living, and whether your entry will bring benefits or competition to that club. Sure, anyone can start a business and earn a living, but to prosper and flourish, that is a different *club*.

Regardless of what the textbooks and the business professors tell you about building a successful business and creating a winning strategy, that only happens in a fairy tale world. In the real world, private conversations will be held within the Old Boys Club to determine your eligibility. Your applications will be tied up waiting for approval for months. Your international suppliers will be contacted behind your back to cut off your supply. Your products will be stuck in the port waiting for clearance and you will be asked to jump through one hoop after another. Somewhere along the process, an official may insinuate that things can be sped up with a cash payment, and the list of stumbling blocks goes on and on. While all this is happening, you will probably be told to dig deeper and work harder.

If you create a business plan based on a perfect environment without consideration of the actual hostile business environment you are going to encounter, you will face many frustrations and worse, you may financially ruin yourself. Unfortunately, many small business owners, solo entrepreneurs and creatives never fully understand the level of what they are up against and continue fighting the same fight day in out, using the same strategies. The years take its toll, and they are left despondent. Some give up while some continue only to merely keep their heads above water.

I had firsthand experience of this while in the setting up stage of the agribusiness. At one point, I had reached out to the senior manager of a quango with the aim of securing shelf-space for my product. Weeks after leaving samples and my contact information and being told a few times they had not had time to consider, I decided to return for the samples and indicated they could reach out to me once they had time to make a decision. A few hours after collecting the samples I had left, I received an email from my international supplier indicating they had received a query from the island with regards to placing an order, and they forwarded it to me. That query was from the senior manager of the quango whose office I had left a few hours ago, after being told they had not had time to decide. You see, I had secured the exclusive rights for distribution to the island and all queries and orders were passed onto me through the suppliers. Obviously, the senior manager was unaware of this.

How I ended up with exclusive rights was based on an unpleasant conversation I had with a seasoned businessperson while in the initial stages of setting up the agribusiness. I could easily have been disheartened but instead, I realised that if I had not secured my business idea, I would have been dead in the water.

In these business environments, there are sectors which are almost closed categories for some, as the invisible rules are there to protect certain individuals, as competition against these players will not be tolerated. Hence why there are so many businesses in the same market vying for a small piece of the pie. These entrepreneurs sell products and services which are non-essential, and they will always struggle in a contracted economy. While there is a high level of dominance with services and products that are considered necessities, the hidden oligopolies continue to thrive.

If you are going to have any chance of surviving and thriving in this type of environment, you need to build a business that can manoeuvre the rough waters. We buy insurance to litigate the risk of life's 'what-if' situations, and the same applies to business. Your business strategy must include a plan of action that mitigates operating in an unfair and hostile business environment.

Create a business in a particular niche and try to secure that business with exclusive rights, trademarks, copyrights, and any other legal frameworks. Know that if you create a business that cannot be secured in that way, it will only be a matter of time before it is replicated. Design a strategy to manage that possibility from the outset. Determine how you will survive the competition when it shows up to the market and how you will retain your customers and clients to ensure longevity in your business. Also, know what your exit strategy will look like.

START-UP CAPITAL

All businesses need some level of start-up capital. Whether you are building a business on a shoestring budget or have access to unlimited capital, you should ensure you have created a cash flow projection.

Start-up capital is invested to bring a return on that investment. While this process is occurring, real-life is still happening. One of the biggest mistakes first-time business owners make, is assuming that the business will generate enough money to maintain them during the start-up phase. Theoretically, the money initially generated is best served being reinvested in the company to maintain its stability and increase the chances of its longevity.

Therefore, one should have formulated a plan to be able to maintain themselves and their personal commitments while the business is in this infancy phase; and chances are, the timeframe within which the company begins to pay a consistent pay cheque to its owner may be twice as long as what was initially imagined.

This revelation may lead you to understand that if you want to give the business the best opportunity of survival and not straddle yourself with risky debt, you may have to maintain a level of employment (whether full or part time) until you can take the full plunge into being a full-time business owner.

"Taking time ain't laziness." Some of the most successful companies are not the ones which were initially the best in the market. Rather, they are the ones which were able to formulate an effective strategy and outlive their competitors.

Think about some of the major brands which have been around for twenty years or more, and you will realise many have gone through growth and image revamp to be where they are now. Of course, there are also many successful companies which were enjoying great success but are no longer around.

Business Start-Up Checklist

Pre Start-Up

- [ ] 1. Decide type of business you are going to start
- [ ] 2. Decide on business structure (business name, limited company, partnership)
- [ ] 3. Create business plan including financial projections, market research and marketing plan

Administrative

- [ ] 1. Choose 3 potential business names and research meaning in different languages
- [ ] 2. Register business
- [ ] 3. Engage lawyer to create legal framework
- [ ] 4. Register with statutory authorities (tax, licenses and permits, employees)
- [ ] 5. Secure business insurance

Business Start-Up Checklist

Financial & Human Resources

- [ ] 1. Secure start-up capital
- [ ] 2. Create operational budget and cash flow projections
- [ ] 3. Open bank accounts
- [ ] 4. Set up management information systems
- [ ] 5. Establish employment contracts

Branding and Marketing

- [ ] 1. Create logo, visuals and business cards
- [ ] 2. Create website and social media pages
- [ ] 3. Create marketing plan including launch campaign
- [ ] 4. Create sales plan

PART III

NEW HORIZONS

CHAPTER 10
BUSINESS UNUSUAL

I believe it is safe to say we are currently living a life that has significantly evolved from what it was fifty, thirty or even fifteen years ago. Admittedly, we are living a life that is not the same as it was just *two* years ago—and while there are many who yearn for the "good ole' days", at this point, we should accept that they are not coming back.

While the world has been changing and we have been making good progress on many fronts, the way in which we perceive money, wealth and our habits have not evolved at the same pace.

For the most part, the idea of wealth and financial security in the Caribbean has been stemmed around owning a home. The ideology of *owning a piece of the rock* is implanted into everyone's minds from a very early age. A person's success is marked by whether they own a home and the larger the house, the more successful they are perceived.

As a child growing up in the '80s and '90s, this idea held fast for anyone who lived in an "upstairs and downstairs" house, for those persons were the movers and shakers of society (or so it was thought). As I look back at it now, those people were largely those who had government jobs or jobs that were deemed to be stable and permanent. Today, however, many houses of that stature simply mean that the people who own them have a bigger mortgage than most.

There was a time when someone purchased a house only after they had saved enough money to secure a solid down payment or build their home with funds they had set aside specifically for that purpose. When the funds were depleted, they stopped building until they had saved enough to restart again. In the "now" world, we would rather have a 100% mortgage to acquire our dream house, even if it means we are house-poor. Let me add, I am of the opinion there is no such thing as house-poor, but more that you have a house you cannot afford.

Not only have we now embarked on a road where mortgage debt is strangling homeowners, but these homes are assets that are not performing investments. This theory will trigger many, but let me explain.

An investment is an asset that is attained for the purpose of creating a return, either in the current time or at some point in the future. Investments can be of a short, medium, or long-term nature. A house as an investment property can earn revenue now from rental income, or long-term through an increase in value which is realised when it is sold.

A house, which is used primarily as a residence with no intention of being sold or which does not earn any additional income, is not a performing asset. For the most part, most of the population's house is their primary residence, and while some persons may have additional quarters which are used for earning extra income, many do not. If your home is your biggest investment and fits into the category of a residence home, then your largest asset is not currently a performing asset.

As mentioned in a previous section, for this asset to meet the criteria as a performing asset, with the ability to contribute to the increase of your wealth, it must be kept in a saleable condition. That is, it must be able to be listed in the current state or with minimum touch ups and earn the full market value. While this seems simple, most homeowners do not keep their homes in this kind of saleable state, especially if their intention is to keep the house as their primary home indefinitely. Unfortunately, life sometimes happens, and if that house needs to be sold, the market value is difficult to attain because it has not been maintained or was built with such customised features.

Another reason your house is not a performing asset is the emotion surrounding the investment. Owning a house is almost a passage of rites and signals that the homeowner has achieved one of life's major goals. As long as there is that human emotion attached to the asset, it will not be considered a performing asset, unless the homeowner decides they are willing to sell the house in the future to capitalise on its value.

In years gone by, having most of your wealth wrapped up in your home was one of the best forms of investment. Paying the mortgage would cause the equity to increase and this gave homeowners options if a life emergency arose, or if they needed capital for another venture because they were able to borrow on the equity. Presently, however, most banking institutions are no longer willing to lend on the equity of the home, and the ones that still do, will only allow borrowing of a small percentage on the equity, thereby reducing the homeowner's options.

The other major change is the social aspect of family lives. In years gone by, the house was primarily a family home, and it was not uncommon for different generations to live in the dwelling (especially once the matriarch and patriarch had reached a certain age). That arrangement is not quite the same today, resulting in a more complex financial situation.

As family living arrangements evolve, a few scenarios must be considered.

What happens if the homeowner is no longer able to care for themselves?

What happens if the patriarch or matriarch needs long-term care but one of them is still able to live in the residence?

Previously, family members would cohabit with the elder and contribute to the running of the household, but in the current environment this is no longer the norm.

As the cost of living continues to rise and the fixed income of the retired and the older generation becomes increasingly stretched, the pressure to maintain the household becomes more unattainable. For this reason alone, considering our homes our biggest investment needs to be reassessed. The objective is for one to ensure they have the cash flows in future years to sustain themselves, which also includes the maintenance of their houses.

A safety net of at least 1% of the value of the house should be set aside yearly to adequately maintain it. This can be factored into the budget through sinking funds.

Pension Funds

Aside from the home, traditionally, the next largest investment contributing to a person's wealth was their pension fund. Most private companies now provide this as a benefit to their staff, and for those self-employed persons, creating an individual pension fund has become easier over the years.

When first introduced as part of the remuneration package, they were seen as a way for the average person to maximise and increase their wealth and provide for themselves in their later years. In the earlier days, those plans took between twenty and thirty years to be vested (i.e., the time it took before the individual was entitled to the portion of the funds which were contributed by the company).

During those years, most companies had pension plans which were defined as benefit plans. An employee was guaranteed a specific amount at a particular age, with the calculation taking into account the number of years they had worked and their final salary. To be clear, not all plans used the same basis to calculate final salary. This was quite acceptable as people tended to have a job for life and the longer they stayed, the bigger their retirement pot got.

Fast forward to the present day. Many companies are transitioning away from defined benefit plans as they have become too expensive to maintain, especially with the volatility of the market. With defined contribution plans, an individual is entitled to what they contributed, and once the portion the company has contributed is vested, that is also added. The final payout is dependent on the plan, meaning there is no guarantee of retiring with a specific amount.

Many plans are now vested within two to five years, which is a welcome change in the current working environment. At the same time, defined contribution plans do not offer the same level of security as the defined benefit plan.

The shift in the structure of the plan as well as the uncertainty of the retirement income reduction, is not the only concern one now needs to consider. There is also the reality that pension funds carry a market risk, which many individuals do not consider or understand until they need to. Usually, when they discover that the fund has been compromised (either because of bad investments or because the fund market value has not kept par with the rate of inflation), the amount they receive upon retirement is simply not enough for them to maintain their current lifestyle, and it is too late to make adjustments. There may have been a time when an individual did not need to concern themselves with things they did not understand, because as long as they were contributing to the fund on a monthly basis, the expectation was that it would be there when they needed it.

In the last thirty years, the Caribbean has seen the collapse of insurance companies, commercial banks, and building societies, which resulted in some governments having to step in and bail out these institutions. The ones left holding the bag are the customers whose wealth has vanished before their eyes, and the taxpayers of the countries who are on the hook for the bailout packages. There has been the CL Financial collapse where the financial turmoil was felt across the entire Caribbean and beyond, through the approximately twenty-eight companies it controlled, including Colonial Life Insurance Company (CLICO) and British American Insurance Company (BAICO) and their subsidiaries.

Prior to CLICO, Barbados also saw the collapse of Trade Confirmers and the lengthy, unsuccessful class action suit of the policyholders of Manulife over the demutualisation of the Barbados company. In the mid-'90s in Jamaica, the government also bailed out the finance sector after several commercial banks, societies and life insurance companies were deemed insolvent.

When CLICO Barbados collapsed, I sat in the inaugural meeting of the policyholders and listened to stories ranging from individuals who were two years away from retirement and saw their entire retirement pot disappear, to individuals who had sold a house and decided to temporarily place the funds in a short-term investment option, until it was time to proceed with a new investment. The stories were endless, and each one was more and more heart wrenching. For the most part, these were not individuals whose purpose was to "play the stock market" or who wanted to be active investors. They were not people who bought into the hype and hope of a get-rich-quick scheme. They were everyday persons who simply thought they were being responsible by trying to provide for their future.

When I left that meeting, there were two things I knew for certain. The first was that I was not going to return to another one, and the second was that it could no longer be business as usual. As a result of the fall-out associated with that collapse, people died without being able to access medical care due to not having the resources. People could no longer retire and had to continue working beyond the national retirement age to maintain their lifestyle; and, of course, many could not provide the security to their families from the generational wealth they were trying to amass.

Leaving our future to the decisions of a few, relying on the regulatory authorities to govern these parties and hoping it all works out, is not an option anymore. We must decide to actively manage our financial lives from beginning to end, and this can only be done if we equip ourselves with the necessary knowledge to do so.

You cannot simply rely on a company to look after your retirement plan. Their obligation is not to ensure you can retire at a respectful age with resources to maintain yourself. Their obligation is, firstly, returns to the owners and investors. Yes, it will be in their best interest to look after the working population who produce the effort needed to produce a return on investment, but the onus is on each of us to ensure that the decisions being made are best for ourselves.

Of course, there are levels of data which will be unavailable to the public and not everyone is capable of reading and understanding a set of financial reports from a large corporation, hence the reliance on the regulatory authorities and audited reports. However, at the very basic level, one must know the type of plan they are contributing to, what the maximum contributions are, whether the contribution is being matched by their employer (as well as the maximum they are willing to match), and most importantly, they need to ensure that what they signed up for (including the level of risk), is being reflected in their pay slip and information they received.

I have encountered people who do not review their pay slips, way too many times. There are also some who do not understand how taxes and deductions are calculated. As a result, they have no idea if the remuneration they are receiving is correct. Understanding the level of risk involved in the options you have selected for your plan and what it means for your overall wealth, is also necessary.

At the initial setup of a pension plan, an individual will be requested to choose a level of risk. The options will be conservative, balanced, or high return. Those persons whose aim is to maintain the principle amount, are on the risk-adverse side or are closer to retirement age and not wanting to take levels of risk they are uncomfortable with, will choose the conservative option.

Those who may be at the mid-range point in their career and believe they still have time to take some levels of risk but are not prepared to go to the highest level, will consider the balanced risk, and for those persons who are either at the early stage of their careers and believe they have time to take larger risks in anticipation of a larger return, may opt for the highest risk option.

An individual's situation may change when they are at a different career level or if their family-life status has changed. This may also happen if their wealth portfolio mix shifts and objectives are not the same as when they initially enrolled, but they have not made changes to reflect their life-status change.

The other side to this coin is that, whilst theoretically everyone is aware that having a pension/retirement plan adds to their overall value, few persons track the value of the investment and do so alongside their overall investments, to ensure that the asset mix of their total net worth is suitable to achieve their overall financial objectives.

To mitigate the risk of market conditions and financial turmoil we cannot predict or control, the best option we have is to create a portfolio mix and actively manage that mix to ensure we do not have all our eggs in one basket.

A balanced mix can consist of real estate, stock portfolios, cash, pension funds or business ventures. Note that it does not need to include all the above-mentioned items for an individual to be financially successful. Not only does an asset mix help to balance the risk involved, but it also allows an individual to create streams of income from a variety of sources. This facilitates growth and ensures they are less income-vulnerable. This includes passive income.

Passive income is simply money earned while you sleep. It is income earned from doing nothing or very little. It is income you can continue to earn for your loved ones, even after death.

Looking at an individual's financial story in this manner would have only been considered for persons with advanced financial knowledge. This is one of the primary reasons why there is still a large gap between those who have and those who do not. The fact is, this type of financial strategy can be pursued by anyone at any stage of their financial life, simply because it is not rocket science and you do not need to have a bag of money to learn it. Whether or not your lifestyle is the same as a wealthy person's, your *money decisions* should be the same as a wealthy person's. Anyone can learn to intentionally manage their financial life to increase their wealth, and no one should feel intimidated, even if they are starting from ground zero. With the right mindset and the material being delivered in a format that works for them, it is achievable.

Several generations before, the house was financed by various streams of income. The lady of the house may not have had a full-time job. The income of the house was supplemented by dressmaking jobs from the neighbourhood or in the form of baking on the weekends and holidays. That additional income was also used to acquire parcels of land which were then passed onto future generations. In that era, there were not many fancy terms for what was being achieved, but it was the same concept, and that type of economic activity is the reason many working-class families were able to educate their children.

Financial accountability will be the new way forward in this era of *business unusual*. We know that old keys do not open new doors and we know we need new keys because those old ones do not work for the majority of the population. The future's success will be bestowed upon those who are simply brave enough to step out of the current mould and embark on their own journey.

BUILDING WEALTH

Wealth is the accumulation of assets and resources. It is created by having an excess of what you require. Wealth can be inherited. It can also be created and passed onto future generations. For this to happen, it must continue to grow.

How is Wealth Created?

The simplest theory related to creating wealth is to generate multiple streams of income, have a substantial income source, and save the profit. Additionally, one would need to make decisions required to protect the income and savings, and insert a risk factor to grow the money. The final theoretical component requires monitoring and realignment (as needed).

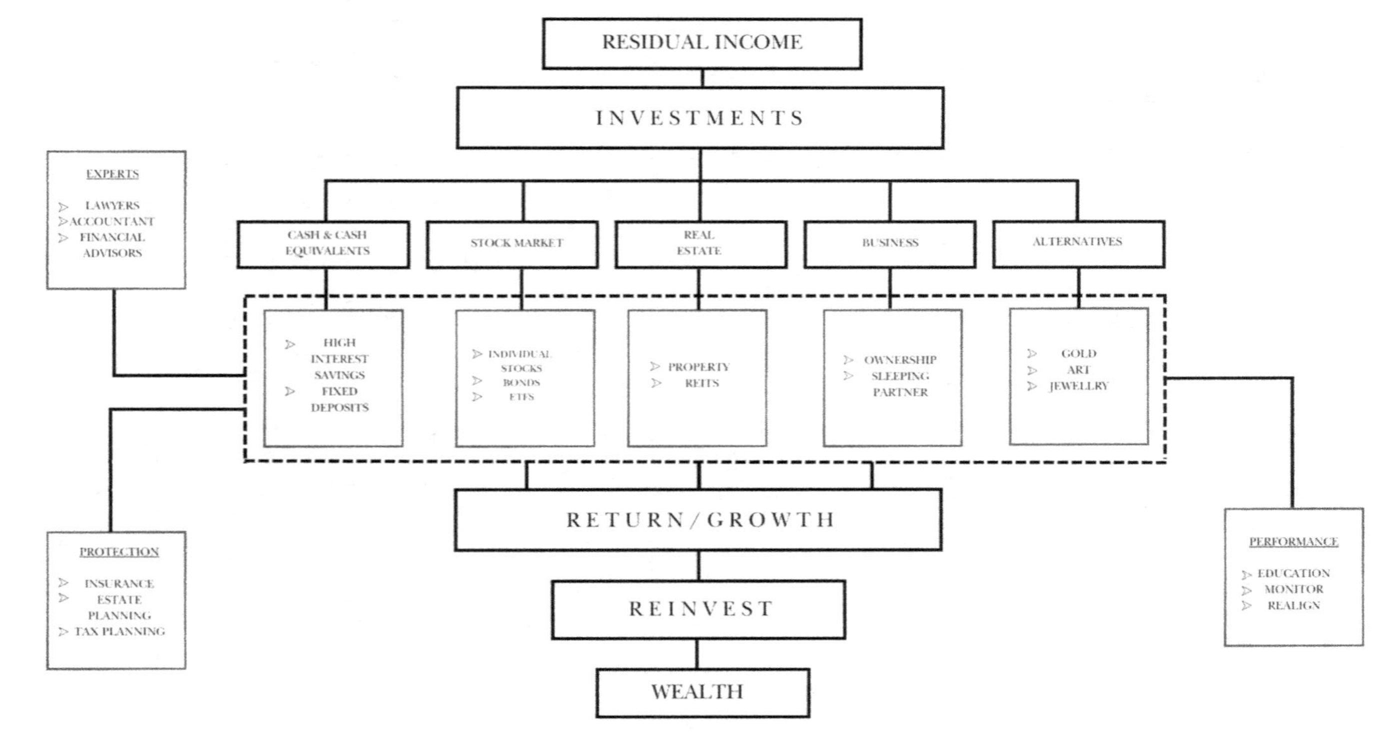

RESIDUAL INCOME
INVESTMENTS
EXPERTS
LAWYERS
ACCOUNTANT
FINANCIAL ADVISORS
CASH & CASH EQUIVALENTS
STOCK MARKET
REAL ESTATE
BUSINESS
ALTERNATIVES
HIGH INTEREST SAVINGS FIXED DEPOSITS
INDIVIDUAL STOCKS
BONDS
ETFS
PROPERTY
REITS
OWNERSHIP
SLEEPING PARTNER
GOLD
ART
JEWELLRY
PERFORMANCE
EDUCATION
MONITOR
REALIGN
PROTECTION
INSURANCE
ESTATE PLANNING
TAX PLANNING
RETURN/GROWTH
REINVEST
WEALTH

Protecting your income and savings will involve insurance policies, estate planning, advice on tax matters and any other measures needed to guarantee that the wealth does not evaporate. These protections also ensure that it can be carried onto the next generation.

As previously mentioned, growing your wealth will involve some level of risk. Monies left in a bank account for an extended period will only generate a minimum amount of interest. Using another investment method, such as the stock market, real estate or a business, can generate larger returns; however, there must be a balance between higher returns and the risk involved. Higher risk does not always equate to higher rewards, and one will have to consider their personal risk-appetite.

Monitoring your portfolio is a necessary process to ensure the decisions made are leading to an increase in wealth. When you begin to monitor the value of your assets, you will have a clearer picture of the assets which are performing, and the ones which are not. When making improvements to your home, does it increase the value of the property? These are the types of scenarios which indicate whether you are going in the right direction and facilitate the decision-making process.

Monitoring also includes keeping updated information as it relates to the various methods of protection. There are many tragic examples for us to learn from. For example, individuals who, at the time of their death, had not updated the beneficiaries on their insurance policies, thus leaving their loved ones in precarious situations which result in drama and lawsuits; or an untimely event (such as a fire) for the homeowner to realise they had not updated the value on their policy as they made improvements to their home. It can be heart wrenching to discover that the protection you need in those moments is not available, despite believing you have been responsible all along.

Creating and assuming wealth will require skill sets that may be above your competence, and you should not hesitate to solicit the assistance of professionals to help you make the best financial decisions for you and future generations.

BUYING BACK YOUR FREEDOM

We are now trapped in an extremely fast-paced world and many of us pride ourselves in our ability to keep pace. Somewhere along the way, that requirement made its way into job descriptions and, many days, we are nothing more than hamsters on a treadmill.

A sizable portion of the population's life currently centers around work, both inside and outside of the home. Even for those fortunate enough to have assistance with some of their daily tasks and demands, time to properly relax and partake in activities we are passionate about, continues to be limited.

By the '90s, 74% of women were working outside the home. This was in addition to 93% of men who comprised the working population. This reality created an increase in economic benefits for everyone, as well as a demand on time. A shift from a maximum of forty hours per week, to a minimum of forty hours per week, has left little time for the other affairs of life.

In some parts of the world, the introduction of paternity leave, increased time-off for working mothers, and flexi-time, and now remote-working has been welcomed, but for much of the working population (and certainly in the Caribbean), none of this is close to reality.

Add to this the increased cost of living, the perpetual pay-gap between men and women, the pressure of not forfeiting upward mobility by taking career breaks, the stress of the work environment, as well as the stress these scenarios place on family life, and it is no wonder more and more people are looking for ways to escape the rat race.

As Maya Angelou said: "My mission in life is not merely to survive, but to thrive; and to do so with some passion, some compassion, some humour, and some style."

Buying back your freedom allows you to choose the work you are most passionate about, in the environment that works best for you, with the ability to do whatever, whenever, while decreasing your stress level and living a healthier lifestyle.

Buying back your freedom may mean working fewer hours, not working at all, or changing career paths. It could also mean freeing yourself in other ways, like abandoning consumerism and living in a world of *less*. Every item we own represents a decision we made at some point and takes up space, not just physically but also mentally. Understand, there is a maintenance cost for all this physical and mental baggage.

If you won the lottery tomorrow, would you continue to live your life the same way, spending the same number of days and hours at work, commuting, in meetings, cleaning and tidying and all the other jobs that occupy your time now?

Sure, you may love your career and/or your job and colleagues, but there is a high probability that if you won the lottery, one of the first changes you would make is how you utilise your time. By acknowledging this, then you can focus on buying back your freedom. Buying back your freedom takes you on the path to financial independence. In theory, your bills will be paid without you getting out of bed.

Like everything else, there are various versions of what this looks like and you are invited to choose the one that works best for you.

For those who want to fully *fire de wuk* and live a life of leisure, they have the option of scaling back their expenses and living a frugal, minimalist lifestyle. This will allow them the luxury of not having to go to work. This type of path can be considered lean financial independence. With this path, the idea is that people can pay their basic living expenses and are willing to forfeit most of life's luxuries to be able to secure their freedom. Lean financial independence can be attractive to those who may not necessarily want to retire early but do not want to wait until they are sixty-five (or older) to do so. These people tend to be well-versed in budgeting and organisation and know how to save a dollar. They have life skills which can be used to maintain this kind of lifestyle.

For those who want to continue their current standard of living after *firing the wuk*, they will follow a path of regular financial independence. This path will see them continuing to enjoy vacations and even owning luxury vehicles after retiring. Persons on this path, would have worked to ensure they not only saved for their retirement, but that they invested those funds into areas which will continue to provide passive income, thus allowing them to maintain their lifestyle. These people will have spent time equipping themselves with the knowledge needed to make sound investments and are capable of maintaining a financially sound path.

Persons who wish to continue to work, albeit at a slower pace or with equal time off, may choose to continue to work part time. This style is similar to the barista concept of financial independence. It is attractive to people who have already secured themselves financially and now have the choice to scale back their hours or switch to a less lucrative career which aligns with their passion. They continue to work part time either because they want to remain active, and/or they feel more secure knowing they are covering their annual expenses and not relying solely on their investments; or there are benefits from their employment they want to continue enjoying, such as family medical benefits. In some countries, the cost of good medical insurance is rising to levels that are unmanageable by retired persons.

To secure your path to freedom, the first step is living a financially responsible life. This is where you have acquired the financial knowledge you need and have mastered the art of budgeting.

Step two involves getting out of debt, since the funds going towards paying debt interest are best saved and invested to earn a return. Carrying debt into retirement is risky business and will make you financially fragile. I am not only referring to inflation risk, but also to that of market changes, which may impact the cost of the debt, and is possible with variable loan rates. There is also the risk that a person's income may decline because of lower dividends from investments, or even from the loss of real estate rental income from a downturn in the economy. With so many possibilities over which you have no control, going into retirement with a debt-free slate is best.

The third step to financial freedom involves savings and investing. This is where the decision on what path of freedom you choose will come to light. The idea of regular financial independence may be the objective until one realises the amount of money it will take. At that point, they may decide to choose another path.

Here is 's a simple calculation of what financial freedom may look like:

Yearly living expenses * estimated remaining life expectancy

=

financial freedom (adjusted for inflation rate)

At the age of fifty, and based on living until the age of three scores and ten (seventy years), then the number of years to provide for would be twenty years. At a yearly rate of $50k for living expenses, then financial freedom begins at $1M before adjusting for inflation. This does not mean you will need to save $1M beforehand, but it provides an idea of how much you will need to live out those twenty years given what you have saved and your future income. Of course, seventy years is the median life expectancy estimate, as many people now enjoy a full life well beyond that age, and that needs to be considered as well.

Step four involves creating passive income to replace (or partially replace) your employment income.

Buy Back Your Freedom

Step 1 – Be financially responsible
Step 2 – Get out of Debt
Step 3 – Savings and Investing
Step 4 – Passive Income

Passive income is not limited to only persons who have investments or start-up capital to use. People can use their knowledge to create passive income with little or no start-up capital by creating **digital products,** such as e-books, music, advertising (blog), courses, or artistic prints. With these options, you create the package to be sold once and can continue to sell for years with a bit of follow-up promotion over those years. This type of passive income, as it is unique to you, will also be a bit more difficult for competitors to replicate.

Another type of passive income which involves using **intellectual property** (that is, from the talents and experience you already have), includes music royalties, patents, books and trademarks. Patents and trademarks are areas where there is a tendency for them to be left unsecure, leaving the opportunity for others to capitalise on products and services you have spent years producing. By securing your intellectual product, you can create another stream of passive income using your creations.

Paid Directorships are another source of income which can be earned utilising your experience in a particular area with minimum effort. This usually involves periodically attending meetings and engaging in other business tasks. That is, of course, if you can secure them, because let us face it - they are hard to come by.

One of the most spoken about types of passive income is that which is derived from **stock and cash investments from dividends and interest paid.** This is dependent upon having funds to invest upfront and on choosing the right investments which will offer a return, however, can be started with as little as $100, and by utilising their spare time, an individual can acquire the skills to get themselves started.

Another area which may not require large amounts of initial outlay is **investing in a business** as a sleeping partner. There are always individuals seeking start-up capital for their small business and, with some research and a legal framework in place, this can be a feasible option. The legal agreements entered into would highlight the levels of profits you are entitled to. You can also create a business and hand it over to a manager with minimum daily input from you. As the owner of the business, you would enjoy the benefits of the return on profit.

Peer-to-Peer lending either through a registered company or as an individual is also another source of income that can be achieved without substantial amounts of outlay. Peer-to-Peer lending is when an individual with excess savings who is interested in earning a return on that money is matched with an individual who is desirous of borrowing money. Details as it relates to interest rates, duration of loan and repayment schedule would be established at the outset.

The most coveted type of passive income is that of real estate, as it can provide income that has the potential to replace your income. It can be considered a reliable source of revenue which you can retain for many years with the goal of passing it to future generations.

Passive income from real estate can be in the form of monthly or yearly rent received. There is also the unrealized increase in value, which will come to fruition once the investment has been sold. For example, while you are receiving rental income from your real estate investment, the value of the building can also increase based on additions, market fluctuations or even the location. This increase would be considered realised when the property is sold. A house purchased for $250k, currently valued at $300k, would have an unrealised value of $50k.

Real estate passive income requires a considerable outlay of cash and time to start, and depending on the type of model chosen, there may be quite a bit of work to service and maintain. However, these activities can be outsourced once the property is established.

This list is by no means exhaustive, and there are many other options for investment income which require more effort to manage daily, and therefore do not correspond with the true definition of passive income. Financial independence does not require that every type of income is of a passive nature. Therefore, other options can be pursued.

CHAPTER 11
FIVE LIFE LESSONS

The journey of life demands that we learn some lessons along the way. Some lessons are hard, some are enlightening, and some are not even our own. We can apply these lessons to any area of our life and in this final chapter, I will share five, which can translate from everyday life to our financial story and can help keep us grounded.

Lesson #1 - Shit happens

Businesses fail, markets crash and investments disappear. Breadwinners die, chronic sickness rears its head. It is inevitable that as long as we are alive, there will be one challenge or another. Some are manmade and are outside the realm of our control. Life is made up of seasons, and there are times where our financial decisions are going to be tested more than we wish, and like all seasons, this too shall pass. However, for it to pass, it means we must have measures in place to weather those storms and we must be able to stay the course.

The ability to weather the storms may require the use of emergency funds, but those may not be enough of a safety net for the long-term.

Safety nets are there to catch us when our worlds turn upside down. They are there to help us navigate the scariest of times.

Safety nets are not universal. In some countries the public healthcare services are of such a high quality that they can catch those with life-altering health challenges and even provide after care. In other countries, individuals know that they need to be their own safety net as it relates to their health.

A solid financial strategy will need to include those safety nets to cushion the blows of life, should the need arise. Private medical insurance, life insurance, long-term disability, and retirement plans are all safety nets. Many of these are offered as part of employment packages for some, but there are many who still do not enjoy these kinds of benefits. Even in companies where these are offered, the level of coverage is based on a person's seniority and compensation. Some higher levels of insurance are only afforded to the senior executives of a company, and therefore an individual may not have enough coverage to manage their exposure.

Assessing your personal situation, determining what safety nets are required and updating these as the need arises, should be factored into part of your yearly financial plan. An insurance policy bought twenty-five years ago for a single individual, certainly does not satisfy the needs of a family of four in the current environment. Likewise, decisions may have been made twenty-five years ago based on the limited information one had, which is now irrelevant for the lifestyle they wish to pursue.

One may have come to the realisation that a particular safety net does not actually catch them and decide not to keep all their eggs in one basket. They may want to break away from the traditional safety nets. For the many people who have lost life savings and investments in the economic crashes, and due to the demise of insurance companies over the years, they certainly will want to look at what may be considered unorthodox types of safety nets.

Two years away from retirement, hearing that the insurance company holding your retirement fund has folded, and that there is no recourse, is not something anyone imagines will ever happen to them. However, over the last thirty years, the instances of this happening have occurred frequently enough for individuals to really start thinking about other methods of protecting themselves. While no one method will be foolproof, statistically, you are better off using a few methods as opposed to considering only one option.

Lesson #2 - No One Cares

A lesson people learn too late in life is that very few people really care about them or their life decisions. Many get involved when there is nothing else to occupy their time. As Bajan old folks would say, "Talk last for three days," meaning, people will talk about you for a period of time and they will move on to whatever is the latest topic.

Your business may not prosper the first time. You may go through years of living on a bare-bones budget while trying to change your financial life, and that is okay. Sometimes the path you choose does not always work out and you need to adjust your sail or abort the mission altogether and start over. Life does not come with an instruction manual, and what works for one does not necessarily work for another. The best gift we can give ourselves is the gift of trying. Being preoccupied with other people's opinions and what they may say should not be your priority, because whether you are doing good or bad, someone will have an opinion.

Unfortunately, people find themselves falling into the trap of thinking others really care about their life decisions, only to wake up decades later and realise they were on a path that was leading nowhere. Instead of having the boldness to get off that path, they stayed on it because of what people might say, only to realise (or *never* realise) there is no one there to say anything because they have long moved on.

Picking up a second job, selling the car you cannot afford, going back to school - whatever you need to do to secure your financial future - is on you because in the end, it is you who needs to care.

Lesson #3 - It's All Just Stuff

In the end, it is all just stuff. The experiences will remain with us, and the rest will eventually end up in a landfill, whether in our lifetime or the lifetime of the generations who come after us, who will not see the value in the items.

If you have ever spoken to someone who has lived a long life or someone who is at the end of their life, they do not wish for a bigger house, a more expensive car or more expensive clothing; and while they may reminiscence about their early days, the memories of the material items and their cost have faded. That, in and of itself, should warn us that "stuff" should add to our happiness, but our happiness or level of success should not be determined by how much of it we have been able to accumulate.

Sometimes we attach more value to items than they are worth. I remember being on the verge of moving countries after my first expat experience. When I requested a quote from a shipping company and saw how much it cost to ship items across continents, the things which were of value became a lot clearer to me. There are, of course, items which may hold sentimental value to us and those are the ones we treasure most, but for the most part, the rest is just stuff which can be upgraded, replaced, or forgotten.

Years ago, I came across the topic of *döstädning,* also known as *Swedish death cleaning,* and I found the concept fascinating. It is the process of decluttering before you die to make things less tedious for your loved ones. By doing this, people also know what items were sentimental to you. This concept may be a bit morbid to some; however, it can help you in your day-to-day living and in keeping your home decluttered.

Lesson #4 - Health and Money

We often hear that 'health is wealth', meaning without our health we are nothing. It does not matter how much money you have when you are diagnosed with a rare, end-stage cancer, or some other kind of long-term illness and death is inevitable. Successful individuals who have accumulated wealth over the years, as well as those who aspire to do so, know this, hence why they are intentional about their daily healthy habits, both physical and mental. This is because they know it not only contributes to longevity, but it also allows their minds to focus on their daily tasks.

But let us talk about the effect that lack of money and constant worry about debt and poor lifestyle because of living below the poverty line, can have on one's health. People who are in a constant state of money worry develop poor sleeping habits from tossing and turning at night, and without decent sleep, the body will eventually break down. The body can also be physically broken from the exhaustion of constant work, taking on additional shifts, a second job to make ends meet, or working excessive hours to prove your worth due to fear of job loss.

Long-term money stress also affects mental health as the body is in a constant heightened state (fight mode), waiting for the next penny to drop, debt collectors, unpaid bills, or unexpected sickness. It can always feel as if there is going to be another monster waiting around the corner. This constant worry then brings on illnesses in the body, creating more stress as one is unable to work or function at full capacity, which causes more money problems. The cycle seems never-ending.

Living in this state for years takes a toll, which culminates in anxiety and depression. Even when an individual manages to pull themselves from the state of money problems, the anxiety can translate into emotions which manifest in hoarding or spend-a-holic activities.

Research shows children who are subjected to this type of upbringing, where money is a constant worry or having to go without their basic needs, such as meals being met, will carry its effects through to adulthood unless they intentionally address the issues.

The report, *Does Money Affect Children's Outcomes: An Update* from the London School of Economics and Political Science (LSE), highlighted that income itself is important for children's cognitive development, physical health, and social and behavioural development. Children with delayed cognitive development will struggle with decision making and will tend to make poorer financial choices as adults.

It is one thing to be unable to have the same latest gadgets as their friends, but not knowing if they are going to have a meal the next day or where they are going to lay their heads that night should never be a burden a child has to bear.

Money woes affect relationships with our partners and children, as the worry leads to anger and frustration. Statistics show that 22% of marriages end in divorce over money and 78% of couples admit to arguing over it. Individuals are more likely to stay in relationships where they are experiencing abuse if they do not have the means to financially support themselves or if their standard of living will drastically decline by severing the union. All this leads to more stress and strain on the body. If for no other reason than maintaining a healthy mind and body, it is important we take charge of our financial life.

. . .

LESSON #5 - When Is It Enough?

"When I get a better job, and a bigger house..."

"When I reach \$1M... (wait, that's not enough in today's market) maybe \$3M..."

And the list goes on.

Contentment is the place at which you express gratitude for how much you have achieved and are comfortable and happy where you are. It does not mean you are looking for a rocking chair to wilt away. You can still have goals; however, your validation is not wrapped up in titles, material things, or a dollar value.

The journey of life has many roads and if you have truly started from the bottom, then you probably have had a wild ride. The twists and turns, hills and valleys will, no doubt, have a major impact on who we ultimately become by the time we reach our destination (whatever that destination is). It is easy to lose yourself along the journey and arrive at your destination hardened and aggrieved, or you will struggle with knowing where that destination is, because the ghost of the past keeps you on the go, making you believe it is never enough. If you do not take the time to find your peace and heal from the struggle of the journey, no number of accolades or dollar value will ever be enough.

Money is not the root of all evil. The *love* of money is.

Money does not make you happy, but neither does poverty.

Money will not solve all the problems of the world, but *with* money we can solve many.

Money will not make you feel good about yourself, but you can use money to pay a good therapist to understand why you do not.

Money will not stop racism, but it is fun watching people wait for another elevator in a luxury hotel.

We all need money to reach our true potential and live the life we deserve. Our lives should not be determined by where we were born or the resources that were bestowed upon us at birth. By accepting responsibility for our financial lives, we can truly Live Loud and unapologetically, albeit on a budget.

EPILOGUE

I am approaching you from my current self. Why my current self? Because as I look back on this piece of writing, there is a part of me that I do not recognise or identify with any longer; however, I beam with pride at that girl and how far she has come.

Let me state, this book is not meant to be a guide. It should be seen as encouragement to live your true, authentic life, and a medium to stimulate your ideologies.

When I began writing this book, I simply wanted to write about personal finances to help people manoeuvre the world of finance in a way that would help them live their best life. This is because I have always felt my ability to harness my financial life, has afforded me the opportunity to be *my* authentic self. What I had not anticipated was that writing this book would be cathartic.

Growing up on the island of Barbados, I played the hand I was dealt, and I never thought too much about that hand. I knew the life I wanted to experience, and my decisions reflected that. Where I started was no different from what I saw around me, and what the societal norms were at the time. According to Caribbean elders, if you wanted a future, you went to school and learned.

In retrospect, having been around the world and back (not just as a travel experience but as an individual who has spent the majority of the last fifteen years abroad or on the road, setting up home in five additional countries, with the distinguished pleasure of gaining insight into the lives of people from various cultures and religions), I now see my own, especially my earlier years from a new perspective. I also see where I diverted from the societal norms I witnessed during my formative years, to create my own path and unlearn some of those traditional behaviours.

A bright eyed twenty-two-year-old living on her own with adult decisions and bills, working up to twelve hours a day, teaching herself ACCA at night and paying for it out-of-pocket felt normal. I clearly was not processing the magnitude of it all at the time because I never felt overwhelmed, deprived, and certainly did not miss the parties. During those years, I was also heavily involved in community service with an international service organisation.

In hindsight, it was during that time I mastered the art of time management, being organised, disciplined and most importantly, financial authenticity. My cheques went where I wanted them to go. I did not try to keep up with the Jones', and I never embraced debt. I was certainly living my then version of my best life.

This piece of writing is a reflection of the journey it took to get where I am today. I am a firm believer that if we take away the challenges and the not-so-nice parts, we will not arrive at the beautiful places. Arriving at the beautiful place is the reason we need to keep pushing away from the not-so-nice parts, for the challenges should not be in vain.

I do not profess to have it all figured out, because on any given day I have no idea what I am doing, and I am okay with that.

Because I am enjoying the journey. What I do know, is that financial freedom and independence are the destination and when I have deemed myself to have fully arrived there, I will come back to tell you all about it... from my hammock.

ABOUT THE AUTHOR

Tanja was born and raised on the island of Barbados. At the age of fourteen, she chose accounting as her profession and is now a Fellow of the Association of Chartered Certified Accountants. With twenty-five years of experience in the corporate world, which spans various industries, including international business, insurance, and hospitality, she has built a reputation as a budget guru.

Her life as an expatriate began fifteen years ago and, to date, she has lived and worked in five countries garnering a wealth of experience. She uses these real-life experiences, and those from her solo trips across the world to over forty countries where she mostly engaged in off-the-beaten-track type experiences, in her writings.

Ten years ago, Tanja began using her skills to assist individuals in their quest to better manage their monies and reach their financial goals through one-on-one coaching. An advocate and practitioner of debt-free living, she guides individuals to the life they desire through smart financial choices.

When Tanja is not speaking on financial matters or trekking around the world, she can be found gardening or learning a new skill, as food security and self-sustainability are important to her. She believes the ability to tap into one's talent is tantamount to writing a cheque for oneself.

For more information, visit her website: **www.tanjagittens.com** or **www.livingloudonabudget.com**.

BIBLIOGRAPHY

Bean Underhill, Edward, *Life of James Mursell Phillippo: Missionary in Jamaica*, Yates & Alexander, 1881

Caribbean Development Bank, *The Changing Nature of Poverty and Inequality in the Caribbean: New Issues, New Solutions*, 2016

Central Bank of Barbados, *The 2019 Financial Stability Report*, 2019

Chase, Noel, Barbados' Debt Crisis: *The Effects of Colonialism & Neoliberalism, University at Albany*, State University of New York, 2019

Cooper, Kerris & Stewart, Kitty, *Does Money Affect Children's Outcomes? An Update*, London School of Economics, 2017

Davis, Christopher G, & Mantler, Janet, *The Consequences of Financial Stress for Individuals, Families, and Society*, Carleton University, 2004

Draut, Tamara & Silva, Javier, *Borrowing to Make Ends Meet, The Growth of Credit Card Debt in the '90s, Demos*, 2003

Goddard-Durant, Sadie K, *"Resilience" in Barbados: Bein' uh work in Progress*, (Doctoral dissertation, University of Guelph), The Atrium, 2019

Henriques, Fernando, *Colour and Contemporary Society in the Caribbean*, 1969

Housel, Morgan, *The Psychology of Money: Timeless lessons on wealth, greed and happiness*, Harriman House, 2020

John, Tamanisha J, *Settler Colonialism and Financial Exclusion of Banks in the English Caribbean*, 2018

Sharples, Jason T, *Slavery and Fear*, Oxford Bibliographies, 2018

Smith, Robert Washington, *Slavery and Christianity in the British West Indies*, 1950

Bibliography

Stanley, Thomas J & Danko, William D, *The Millionaire Next Door*, RosettaBooks LLC, 2010

Appendix

Templates available at www.livingloudonabudget.com

DATE	DETAILS	CATEGORY	TOTAL
TOTAL			$

MONEY IN	BUDGET	ACTUAL
EARNINGS		
ADDITIONAL INCOME		
TOTAL INCOME		

MONEY OUT	BUDGET	ACTUAL
AUTOMOBILE (GAS, INSURANCE, TAXES, REPAIRS)		
BANK CHARGES (FEES, CC ANNUAL FEE)		
BILLS (CELLPHONE, CABLE)		
CLOTHING		
CHILDREN (CLOTHING, SCHOOL FEES, SPORTS)		
DINING & ENTERTAINMENT		
GROCERIES		
HEALTHCARE (INSURANCE, DOC VISITS)		
HOBBIES (SPORTS, BOOKS, GYM)		
HOUSING (RENT, MORTGAGE, TAXES, INSURANCE)		
MISCELLANEOUS (EMERGENCY FUND)		
PERSONAL CARE (TOILETRIES, COSMETICS, SPA)		
TAXES		
TRAVEL & HOTEL LODGING		
UTILITIES (ELEC, GAS, PHONE, GAS, INTERNET)		
LOANS (STUDENT, MEDICAL)		
TOTAL EXPENSES		

SINKING FUNDS	BUDGET	ACTUAL
HOUSE REPAIRS		
BIRTHDAYS		
CHRISTMAS		
TRAVEL		
CAR		
MAINTENANCE		
EVENTS		
BIRTHDAYS		

SAVINGS	BUDGET	ACTUAL
SAVINGS ACCOUNT		
RETIREMENT ACCOUNT		
INVESTMENTS		
TOTAL SAVINGS		

MONEY LEFT OVER	BUDGET	ACTUAL

MONEY IN	BUDGET	ACTUAL
EARNINGS		
ADDITIONAL INCOME		
TOTAL INCOME		

LOANS/MORTGAGES	TOTAL O/S	MONTHLY PMTS	YRS TO REPAY	DEBT RATIO	ACTUAL	MARKET
Mortgage						
Loan #1						
Loan #2						
Credit Card						
Store Card						
TOTAL EXPENSES						

MONEY LEFT OVER	BUDGET	ACTUAL
TOTAL EXPENSES		

LIVING *LOUD* ON A BUDGET

EMERGENCY PANTRY LIST

STARCH

- RICE
- QUINOA
- PASTA   OR
- NOODLES MASHED
- POTATO

PROTEIN

- CANNED BEANS
- CANNED FISH
- EGG WHITES

VEGETABLES & FRUITS

- CANNED FRUIT
- CANNED VEGETABLES
- FRUIT JUICE OR DRINK MIX

BAKING ITEMS

- FLOUR
- DRIED FRUIT
- SWEETENER - SUGAR/HONEY
- CHOCOLATE

OTHER

- OIL
- OAT MEAL/CORNMEAL
- KETCHUP & DRY SPICES
- NUTS & SEEDS
- BOTTLED WATER
- BABY FOOD
- TEA BAGS/COFFEE
- CRACKERS
- DRY CEREAL
- JAM/JELLY/PEANUT BUTTER
- PET FOOD

FREEZER

- MEATS
- FISH
- FROZEN
- VEG BUTTER

DAIRY

- ALMOND MILK/
- CANNED OR POWDER
- MILK
- CHEESE

HOUSEHOLD ITEMS

- PLASTIC CUPS/PLATES & NAPKINS
- TOILET PAPER
- LAUNDRY DETERGENT
- BLEACH OR VINEGAR
- DISHWASHING LIQUID
- CAN OPENER

PERSONAL

- DEODORANT
- BODY SOAP
- TOOTHPASTE
- BODY BUTTER/LOTION
- SANITARY PRODUCTS
- SHAMPOO & CONDITIONER
- BABY PRODUCTS
- MEDICATION (4-6 WEEKS)

HURRICANE LIST

- WATER CONTAINERS
- GASOLINE CONTAINER
- TORCHLIGHT & BATTERIES
- CANDLES & MATCHES
- BATTERY OPERATED RADIO

Index

9 789769 715820